A. L. Rowse was born in Cornwall in 1903. Today a leading historian and man of letters, he went to Oxford as a Scholar in English, and won a Fellowship in history at All Souls. He has written a classic of its kind in *A Cornish Childhood*, with its sequel, *A Cornishman at Oxford*; two portraits of a society with his *Tudor Cornwall* and *The England of Elizabeth*, which also has a sequel in *The Expansion of Elizabethan England*; and a pendant, *The Elizabethans and America*. Two biographical studies, *Sir Richard Grenville and the Throckmortons*, complement each other, while *The Early Churchills* (published in Penguins) and *The Later Churchills* set a model for family history. His gift as a man of letters is displayed in the quartet consisting of his masterly biography, *William Shakespeare*, his edition of *Shakespeare's Sonnets*, *Christopher Marlowe*, and *Shakespeare's Southampton*, with his volumes of essays, *Time, Persons, Places* and *The English Spirit*. As well as his *Cornish Stories*, he has published *A Cornish Anthology* (1968), and *The Cornish in America* (1969), and five volumes of poetry, *Poems of Cornwall and America* being the latest.

The Use Of History

A. L. Rowse

Penguin Books

Penguin Books Ltd, Harmondsworth,
Middlesex, England
Penguin Books Australia Ltd, Ringwood,
Victoria, Australia

First published in the 'Teach Yourself History' series by
The English Universities Press, 1946
Revised edition published 1963
Published in Pelican Books 1971
Revised edition © A. L. Rowse, 1963

Made and printed in Great Britain by
C. Nicholls & Company Ltd
Set in Linotype Pilgrim

This book is sold subject to the condition that
it shall not, by way of trade or otherwise, be lent,
re-sold, hired out, or otherwise circulated without
the publisher's prior consent in any form of
binding or cover other than that in which it is
published and without a similar condition
including this condition being imposed on the
subsequent purchaser

A General Introduction
to the 'Teach Yourself History'
Series

This series has been undertaken in the conviction that there can be no subject of study more important than history. Great as have been the conquests of natural science in our time – such that many think of ours as a scientific age *par excellence* – it is even more urgent and necessary that advances should be made in the social sciences, if we are to gain control of the forces of nature loosed upon us. The bed out of which all the social sciences spring is history; there they find, in greater or lesser degree, subject-matter and material, verification or contradiction.

There is no end to what we can learn from history, if only we will, for it is conterminous with life. Its special field is the life of man in society, and at every point we can learn vicariously from the experience of others before us in history.

To take one point only – the understanding of politics – how can we hope to understand the world of affairs around us if we do not know how it came to be what it is? How to understand Germany, or Soviet Russia, or the United States – or ourselves – without knowing something of their history?

There is no subject that is more useful than history, which is indeed indispensable.

Some evidence of the growing awareness of this may be seen in the immense increase in the interest of the reading public in history, and the much larger place the subject has come to take in education in our time.

This series has been planned to meet the needs and demands of a very wide public and of education – they are indeed the same. I am convinced that the most congenial, as well as the most concrete and practical, approach to history is the biographical, through the lives of the great men whose actions have been so much part of history, and whose careers in turn have been so moulded and formed by events.

The key idea of this series, and what distinguishes it from any other that has appeared, is the intention by way of a bio-graphy of a great man to open up a significant historical theme ; for example, Cromwell and the Puritan revolution, or Lenin and the Russian revolution.

My hope is that as the series fills out and completes itself, a sufficient number of biographies will be produced to cover whole periods and subjects in this way. To give you the history of the United States, for example, or the British Empire or France, via a number of biographies of their leading historical figures.

That should be something new, as well as convenient and practical, in education.

I need hardly say that I am a strong believer in people with good academic standards writing once more for the general reading public, and of the public being given the best that the universities can provide. From this point of view this series is intended to bring the university into the homes of the people.

A. L. Rowse
All Souls College, Oxford

Preface

The whole intention of this book is practical and didactic. It is designed as a statement of the case for the study of history, a discussion of its uses and pleasures, and as a manual of instruction on how to approach the subject.

But though my object has been practical at every point, a historian cannot write a book saying what he really thinks about his subject without developing some general reflections and going into some abstract questions. These are mainly concentrated in Chapter 5. If the reader finds that chapter too uncongenial on a first reading, he should skip it, go on to the end, and then return to it at his leisure. It contains the essence of what I have to contribute on a difficult and important subject.

Short as this book is, it incorporates the experience of many years' teaching and lecturing, thinking and writing about the subject. Nearly twenty years after writing the book I have revised it heavily, rewriting here and there, with the idea of bringing it more up to date and in line with the joint interests of American as well as British readers.

A. L. Rowse

New York, R.M.S. Queen Mary, *April 1962*

1 What is the Use of History?

When I was a boy at school a question that was frequently asked was: *What is the use of history?* And nobody seemed to have any answer. (If the school had been somewhat better, the answer would have been forthcoming all right; for, as I hope to show you, there is a completely satisfactory answer to the question, an overwhelming case for the study of history.)

Nobody had any doubt about the use of science: its utility was stamped upon the face of the subject. You could become a chemist or a physicist or an engineer. But could you become a historian? Even if you could, what did it lead to?

These were no doubt very inadequate modes of thinking; we were only boys at a remote provincial secondary school. But some such modes of thought are current much more widely, if not generally, in the modern world. And what we meant by 'use' was, mainly if not wholly, what use is studying history as a preparation for a career? What kind of job does it lead to? There is a good deal more in the question than that, of course. But even to take it at its most practical and utilitarian, the advantages are by no means so wholly on the side of science as we thought in those days.

Privately, and for myself alone, I very much doubted the use of the weary hours I spent in the physics and chemistry laboratories; what was the use, I thought, of making those horrid smells, of weighing those refractorily ponderable substances, of memorizing those innumerable formulae? For other boys there was some use, and even pleasure, in it. And yet, years afterwards, in a progressive and sympathetic little book on the teaching of science, I find the authors questioning whether there is much educational value in teaching chemistry in schools.

Yet we do not need to question the general use of science and its study for a moment. We are only too well aware of its necessity in an industrial civilization. And beyond the mere question of its utility, in a more profound sense, so far from being anti-science, I am all on the side of the scientific movement of thought which, from the Renaissance onwards, has come to characterize and dominate the intellect of the modern world. History is not in conflict with it ; in the course of the nineteenth century it became part of it. The emergence of the concept of evolution into a central position in thought equally affected science and history, and provided a ground of junction between the two. It is sufficiently realized that the methods of evolutionary science affected the study of history ; what is not so well grasped is that with the theory of evolution history may be said to have permeated the whole conception of science. This interaction, which had such a fertilizing influence upon nineteenth-century thought, has a still more fruitful career before it, if only we can do our duty by the intellectual needs of our time with some fresh thinking.

We are all familiar with the popular slogan that this is a scientific age, but people are not so well aware that it is no less a historically minded age.

These are important themes and they will have their place later on in this book. I cannot expound them now ; I only wish to point out that, in spite of the importance of history for the intellectual outlook of our time, we are in general much less conscious of the need and use of history ordinarily than we are of that of science. Then I wish to return to the practical, indeed utilitarian, approach to the subject.

History has its uses from the point of view of a career, getting a job – apart from anything else it may offer – no less than science ; and these uses may throw some further light on the value of the subject in and for itself.

Let us start with education, with that decisive stage in its progress the transition from school to university, from adolescent to adult life. (We shall deal with history in schools later.) A large number of history scholarships to the university are awarded ; they help to form a major element among arts students in all universities, young or old. So history gives you an open door to the university and an academic career. Afterwards there are the openings for properly equipped teachers of the subject in colleges and schools of all kinds. Around the teaching profession there are certain cultural posts, librarians, archivists, curators of museums, secretaries of institutions, social service workers – now definitely on the increase with the social trends of our time. A more important profession is journalism, with which we may include broadcasting. For political journalists, foreign and military correspondents, it is a great advantage to have had an historical education : so many of the affairs they have to deal with need just that background in order to understand them and make them clear. It is not without significance that some of the most powerful journalists of our time, men who have a large part in forming intelligent opinion on public affairs – such men as Walter Lippman and Henry Steele Commager in ' America, Professor D. W. Brogan and Sir Arthur Bryant in Britain – all have a background of historical study. Their comments would be of less weight if they had not.

Even more important, there is the Civil Service, of increasing importance in all countries today with the growth of the welfare state. History is one of the recognized roads into its higher ranks ; quite rightly, for history gives you the right background for most of the affairs with which you will have to deal in the administrative Civil Service. The work of the Civil Service is for the most part concerned with nothing so pure and abstract as mathematics, but with the administration of human affairs, with the social sciences if you like – for which the appropriate background and training are provided by history.

If history is the appropriate training on the whole for civil servants, it follows that it is indispensable for members of the foreign service, for diplomats and consuls abroad. In all the pitiable revelation of a third-rate mind in a front-rank post that is afforded by a reading of Sir Nevile Henderson's *Failure of a Mission* – he was in a key position as British Ambassador in Berlin from 1937 to 1939 – nothing is more deplorable than the ignorance of the man as to the character of the developments in Germany. Only a little orderly reading of modern

German history would have given him the clue to them. But he seems to have thought a reading of *Mein Kampf* on board ship from South America home was sufficient. No wonder he was both fogged and foxed by the direction of events in Germany and seems never to have grasped it until too late. Nor was he the only one to whom some knowledge of German history would have brought a world of enlightenment. How can one properly understand the career of Hitler and the resurgence of German militarism, its appeal for the German people, if one knows nothing of Bismarck and Frederick the Great, of the whole cult of militarism, the tradition of German aggression? Sir Eyre Crowe at the head of the Foreign Office before the last war understood these things very well; and that is why his formulation of the exigencies of British policy was far more cogent and foreseeing than any subsequent statement of British policy between the two wars. A clearer and more informed view of the situation and its developments might have prevented a second war.

It ought not to have been difficult to forecast, on quite a moderate acquaintance with the German people and their recent history, that they would make a second bid for world-power. The worst thing that their history reveals, worse than the brutality, the stupidity and insensibility, the sycophancy and self-pity, is their lack of any sense of responsibility for what they do – for that is what leads to all the rest. When I lived in Germany for a winter after the war of 1914–18, in a 'good' middle-class household, that of a Lutheran pastor – at a time when revisionists in Britain and America were fatally undermining the peace-settlement – I never heard one word of regret for the war the Germans had precipitated upon the world, with its untold losses in men's lives. All that they regretted was that they had lost it. Even after the second war they loosed upon the world there is little sign that they recognize any responsibility for the disaster they brought upon the world.

That absence of a sense of responsibility, the necessary foundation of any civic sense, runs right through German life from top to bottom and reflects their history. It is the source of most of their misdeeds and misfortunes, for it means a people with great powers of organization and endurance and of brutal strength, but with no moral courage; they are therefore always at the service of any masters who are prepared to drive them forward along the road of aggression to power. Power is the inducement; power is what they worship: little notion that there is anything else that exists in the world of politics. And aggression is the method. After all, aggression is what has usually paid in German history. Frederick the Great's career was one long record of successful aggression. So was Bismarck's. The total upshot of Bismarck's irruption upon the scene was to put back the clock a hundred years in Europe. But the Germans have no sense of that; he did well for Germany, so they thought – and still think, according to Karl Barth, in spite of the immense castastrophe that was the ultimate consequence of his life's work. Yet Frederick and Bismarck have been the two great heroes of politics to the German mind. Politicians might have learned much about modern Germany from the best biographies of Bismarck, by C. Grant Robertson and Eric Eyck.

It was not to be supposed that when the culmination of decades of successful aggression came with their bid for world-power in 1914–18, which so nearly came off and was only scotched in the end, they would not make a second try. All the elements in Germany that stood to gain by war were behind it: the old Junker militarist classes, the landowners, the armaments manufacturers, the big industrialists, large elements of the middle classes, above all the lower-middle class, and the *déclassés* of all types and sections. We received ample warning of what would happen: it was in the books. Anyone who studied them should have known quite well what to expect. There is an ample literature on the history of modern Germany; there is really no excuse for not knowing. But what was so sickening in the years before the war was that none of them seemed to have been read by people in high places, responsible for the conduct of our affairs.* It was indispensable that they should know something of the history of modern Europe.

---

* I have shown something of the fatal consequences for British policy in my book *Appeasement: a Study in Political Decline.*

Britain paid a terrible price for the ignorance of her leaders before the war of the facts and trends of European history. Nor were the isolationists in America any better: America's withdrawal from her proper place in the world-system in 1920 led ultimately to the aggressions of Japan and Germany and the second world war. Now that the United States has the burden and responsibility of leadership of the Western world, the knowledge and understanding of history are more than ever important for her to play her part properly. This means an increasing historical-mindedness on the part of the American people, greater awareness of history among the public, a bigger place for history – for world-history, not merely American history – in education. For political maturity necessitates historical understanding; the latter is a prime component of the former.

Ignorance in high places, and in particular the absence of any historical understanding of the political developments in Europe, led Britain as near as anything to disaster. It is all very well for the circles mainly responsible to blame it now upon the people at large. The people were no doubt ignorant; they always are. But that is no reason why they should continue to be so. I agree with one of the first and noblest of Englishmen, King Alfred, that there is nothing more dangerous than ignorance; as he wrote at the end of his life more than a thousand years ago: 'I know nothing worse of a man than that he should not know.' How right he was! The trouble with human beings has always been not that they ate of the Tree of Knowledge but that they did not eat enough of it.

After two disastrous decades in which the dominant figures in English politics were two Midlands industrialists, what a relief it was to have an historian as Prime Minister. And in spite of what all the mediocrities thought, how much safer! For, as a historian, Sir Winston Churchill knew the underlying long-term exigencies of British policy, the interests of ourselves and the Empire without which we cannot exist. He had them in his bones; they are indeed, one might almost say, in his heredity; for did not Churchill perform for us in our time precisely what his great ancestor, Marlborough, achieved in his?

Take the case of the policy of the Grand Alliance.

That has been the dominating, as it was the necessary, pattern of British policy throughout modern history; when we departed from it we risked, and sometimes experienced, disaster; when we adhered to it we were successful; we were safe, and others along with us. What it means is that when some aggressive power in Europe – Philip II's Spain, the France of Louis XIV and Napoleon, the Germany of William II and Hitler – has become so powerful as to challenge our safety and sometimes the very existence of others, we have banded together with those others in a common alliance to defend ourselves against the overwhelmingly powerful aggressor.

What more natural and right? It is only common sense. It is just what a number of smaller boys would do at school to resist the tyrannies of a bully.

Yet it is extraordinary how that policy – simple and right as it is, in our own interest as well as that of the bulk of other peoples – has been misunderstood and reviled. One can understand the misrepresentations of this policy, and the dislike of its success by some continental historians, a Debidour or a Treitschke – because it defeated the aggressive game of their own particular country, with which they identified themselves. They always put down England's success in forming continental coalitions to Machiavellianism and English gold. It is really very simple and naïf of them; their jealousy blinds their judgement. For with all the Machiavellianism and gold in the world it would have been impossible to form these coalitions, if it had not been in the interest of other peoples as well as ourselves. As a matter of fact, it has usually been even more in other peoples' interest than in our own.

Consider this: as against Philip II and Louis XIV Britain's security was threatened, but hardly her very existence as a nation. That of Holland was. Again with Napoleon, as an island Britain was in a stronger position than other powers; the very independence of most powers of Western Europe was at stake. In our own time, against Germany, our danger has been greater, but not greater than the mortal danger in which France, Poland, Russia, Norway, Denmark, Holland, Belgium, and all central and southern Europe have stood. The fact is that we have a common interest with the great bulk of Europe against an aggressor so powerful as to threaten us all; and that has been the sheet-anchor of our security as a nation in modern times.

It can hardly be a legitimate matter of complaint that this has been very much to our interest. If a power goes clean contrary to its interest it comes to disaster. What is more to the point is that our interest has been compatible with the interest of others, i.e. with the general interest.

Perhaps we may interpolate here how this applies to the United States today. Her policy must in the first instance preserve the interests and maintain the security of the country; but beyond this is the principle of making these objectives compatible with the interests and security of others, at least of the bulk of others. So that the balance of the world-system remains with the United States, and peace is maintained; for other powers, or the bulk of them, do not feel their existence threatened, their liberty of action jeopardized. Contrast the nations of Europe groaning under German tyranny from 1940 to 1944, or of the peoples of eastern Europe under Russian domination today.

Consider too what Britain's earlier role safeguarded: the cultural variety, the astonishing creative fertility and freedom of Europe. If it had not been for that there might have been a succession of uniform patterns imposed by repressive hegemonies upon Europe. We have kept the way open for the infinitely varied contributions of the smaller, less powerful countries to the wonderful creative amalgam that is European culture. There was a time, not long ago, when some Frenchmen regretted Britain's resistance to Napoleon's domination of Europe; they now have had more reason to welcome our resistance to Hitler's. Nor is our historic resistance to continental tyranny ultimately to be regretted by those great powers themselves which have tried to exercise it. Napoleon's immense efforts only exhausted France, and while they were going on they were culturally sterilizing. The deliverance of France from his bondage was followed by a century of the most brilliant achievement in the arts that even France has known. And perhaps the deliverance of Germany from the nightmare of aggressive militarism may have a similar effect of release in the sphere of culture and the spirit.

Of all this that is involved in the policy of the Grand Alliance, of its necessity and the consequences that flow from it, Churchill had a firm grasp that was rooted in history. It was not that he saw the point *ex post facto* – after the facts of the situation had forced Britain back to the old sound tradition of her policy. He saw it all before: his speeches throughout the decade in which we wandered away from it are full of that theme. And it is interesting that it was just during those same years that he was writing his historical masterpiece, *Marlborough: His Life and Times*. Marlborough was the linch-pin of the Grand Alliance that defeated the aggressive designs of Louis XIV and ended his domination in Europe; he was not only its military leader but its brain-centre, its chief diplomatic and executive agent. The career of his ancestor not only affords us a parallel to Churchill's role in defeating Hitler, but it has been a direct influence upon him in performing it.

And how much we owe to him because of it! When the history of this war comes to be written it may well be that an even greater service, if possible, than his part in serving his country in 1940 was that which he rendered in helping to bring into being the great alliance by which alone the fascist powers in Europe and the Far East could be defeated. It was because of this background of thought that he was ready to respond to Hitler's invasion of Soviet Russia with an immediate offer of mutual aid and alliance.

The danger of knowing no history can be brought home even more sharply and simply than over this question of the Grand Alliance. Take the issue of what was happening in Germany in the 1930s, and what was to be expected. Many of our political leaders, and leaders of public opinion, simply did not know what to expect. Churchill knew very well what to expect, though he could not get the people responsible to believe him in time. But then he was a student of history; he had been there before.

Churchill's case provides us with the strongest possible argument for a historical education. He educated himself by studying history; he formed his mind upon it; in the end he became a historian, and wrote one of the finest works of historical scholarship in our time. It is an interesting story; you will find his account of it in his autobiography, *My Early Life*.*

You will already have guessed what I think to be the prime – though not the only – use of history. It is that it enables you to understand, better than any other discipline, the public events, affairs and trends of your time. What could be more important? If you do not understand the world you live in, you are merely its sport, and apt to become its victim. (Most people are that anyway. But that is no reason why you should be one of them. In understanding is our only emancipation.)

For that is what history is about. It is about human society, its story and how it has come to be what it is; knowing what societies have been like in the past and their evolution will give you the clue to the factors that operate in them, the currents and forces that move them, the motives and conflicts, both general and personal, that shape events. It is a study in which you are dealing with human nature all the time; that is where the biographies of great historic figures come in and why it is so useful (besides being very pleasant) to read them. History deals not only with the lives of great individuals; in a sense it may be said to consist of the sediment of the lives of millions of smaller men and women who have left no name, but who have made their contribution. Their lives make the material of history as a coral-reef is built up out of the lives of millions of minute marine creatures.

History is then a social science. In that lies its flexibility, its variety and excitement. It is so much less rigid than physical science, more subtle and appealing to the imagination, for it deals with human beings in all their complexity and incalculability. It is always alive and can be thrilling.

That does not mean that you cannot draw lessons or form

---

* And cf. my essay, 'Mr Churchill and English History', in *The English Spirit*.

generalizations from it. Of course you can, as from ordinary human experience. Only with history you have so much more range of experience to draw on: in fact the whole range of human experience that we know of. And though the individual is apt to be unpredictable (even he is not always), great social groupings, masses of men, classes, communities, nations tend to react in similar ways to similar situations. They give you the ground of history, so to say – the stuff upon which the more intricate and individual patterns have been worked. And so, though you may hardly say that there are historical laws of the regularity and exactness of the laws of physical science, there are generalizations possible, of something like a statistical character. There is no need for a chaotic scepticism with regard to history. The fact that such generalizations and tendencies are more irregular, the movements more complex, is all the more intellectually exciting because of their subtlety. You are dealing all the time with human material; so that you need, above all, common sense, sympathy, imagination to appreciate and understand it.

It is public affairs, public events and movements that give one the indispensable background. That is the truth expressed in the much-discussed dictum of Seeley: 'History is past politics; politics is present history.' It is not that Seeley's saying is untrue – though it is sometimes attacked as if it were – but that it is not exhaustive. It is indeed inadequate; there is so much else in history, as there is in the human experience that is history, besides politics or even social affairs. All the same, society and its affairs set the pattern.

Now you will see why I think history is of the utmost importance at the universities, as a preparation for the teaching profession, the Civil Service, our political leadership in its widest sense, leaders of the press and public opinion, no less than for politicians. A knowledge of history is indispensable to the higher direction of society; that is why it is especially important in higher education, and the higher up the more important.

There is a popular saying that 'history never repeats itself'; and that is sometimes given as a reason for holding that you cannot draw lessons from it. Of course it does not repeat itself in precise detail, for there are never the same persons, the same situations with precisely the same characters again. But that does not mean that there are not similar situations, which similarly handled lead to similar results. Over and over again one notices in the history of revolutions, to take one example, the same kind of crisis crop up, a situation with very comparable elements constituting it, whether it is England in the 1640s, France in the 1790s, or the Russia of 1917; one sees the situation ill understood and worse handled by an old régime feebly directed, whether by Charles I, Louis XVI, or Nicholas II, and the situation get out of hand in much the same manner. It is a point that is made, perhaps too dogmatically – as if almost there were a natural history of revolution – by Trotsky in his *History of the Russian Revolution*. But the general point holds good.

H. A. L. Fisher, after spending some years in writing his *History of Europe*, summed up his view of it in his preface :

One intellectual excitement has, however, been denied me. Men wiser and more learned than I have discovered in history a plot, a rhythm, a predetermined pattern. These harmonies are concealed from me. I can see only one emergency following upon another as wave follows upon wave, only one great fact with respect to which, since it is unique, there can be no generalizations, only one safe rule for the historian : that he should recognize in the development of human destinies the play of the contingent and the unforeseen. This is not a doctrine of cynicism and despair. The fact of progress is written plain and large on the page of history; but progress is not a law of nature. The ground gained by one generation may be lost by the next. The thoughts of men may flow into the channels which lead to disaster and barbarism.

There is a lot of disillusioned Liberalism in that. We need not cavil at the latter half of what Fisher says. But with regard to the first : there is of course no *one* rhythm, or *one* plot, in history. To suppose that there is, or even to expect it and be disappointed, is a relic of the religious view of the universe with its providential ordering of history to a given *terminus ad quem*. Acton's somewhat unilateral view of history as the unfolding story of human freedom – a view very characteristic of the nineteenth century – is in direct line of descent from Bossuet's teleological view of Universal History as leading up to the Christian revelation ; and, paradoxically enough, is in direct line coming from St Augustine, whose emphasis was yet quite contrary to human freedom.

No : there is no one rhythm or plot in history, but there are rhythms, plots, patterns, even repetitions. So that it is possible to make generalizations and to draw lessons. Great men both of action and of intellect have always thought so. That is why history was the favourite reading of Napoleon, as of Lloyd George and Churchill – or for that matter, of Hitler. (He might with advantage have read a little more clearly Napoleon's campaign of 1812 in Russia. But then Hitler was a profoundly *uneducated* man of genius ; there could be nothing more dangerous, with such a criminal mentality in a position of power.) All the ancients, both Greek and Roman, read history not only for pleasure, but for the light it threw upon events and the lessons they could learn from it. So too with the men of the Renaissance : Machiavelli, Erasmus, Thomas More, Bodin, Guicciardini, Bacon, Hobbes, Clarendon. Sir Charles Firth tells us : 'Not only is it a branch of learning to be studied for its own sake, but a kind of knowledge which is useful to men in daily life,' and he quotes Sir Walter Ralegh : 'the end and scope of all history being to teach us by example of times past such wisdom as may guide our desires and actions.' This it is that makes Bacon say when discussing the virtues of different kinds of studies : 'Histories make men wise.'

What kind of lessons are those that history teaches? you may ask. They are indeed innumerable, and of all kinds, personal as well as social. But we are confining ourselves to the most strictly political, the realm in which a knowledge of history is a prime necessity.

Let us take, for example, the truth expressed in the saying that you may expel history with a pitchfork but it always comes back. How revealing that is of the course of revolutions ; you may see it at work in each of the three prime revolutions I have mentioned, the English, the French and the Russian. With the execution of Charles I, Cromwell and his Army made a drastic break with the English past, they scrapped the old monarchical form of government that was deeply entrenched in the nation's experience. It was not long before monarchy came sweeping back again; a few years before, Cromwell himself was offered the kingship, which he could afford to refuse because he was already in possession of more monarchical power than ever the king had had. With the death of the great man the nation went back with relief to its old ways and constitutional forms; the monarchy was restored in the person of Charles I's son and heir – to the general satisfaction. The point is that the Puritan revolution and the dictatorship of the Army formed a departure from the normal courses, the deeply ingrained habits of the nation. It is as if a nation has, by its character and structure, certain norms which govern its conduct and mould its institutions. Usually these are so much taken for granted that they are not in evidence. And in any case few people are so sensitive, or so philosophical, as to be conscious of the very elements in which they live and move. People are never more aware of these elements, these norms, than in the moment of departure from them. Hence the particular self-consciousness, vivacity and value of political thinking in revolutionary periods.

Everyone is aware of how this applies to the French revolution in the Thermidorian Reaction, when the revolutionary impulse had run its course, made profound changes, perpetrated great excesses, and most normal people were very glad to get back to normal conditions. Let us take a new, and particular, instance: the effect of the revolution upon French foreign policy, the attitude of the French to other peoples.

The outbreak of the revolution and its first developments – the fall of the Bastille was a universal symbol – raised the hopes of idealists everywhere to a fever-pitch of excitement. Never can there have been such an upsurge of hope, the confident expectation of a new era for mankind, at any historic event. Not only those who were young, and poets, seem to have thought that it portended a new heaven and a new earth. It must have been delicious to live in that moment, to be borne upon such pinions of enthusiasm. (Such an experience is denied to us, fortunately – for the disillusionment was no less intense.) The mood of the time is expressed in one of the greatest of English poems, *The Prelude* :

> Bliss was it in that dawn to be alive,
> But to be young was very Heaven ! O times,
> In which the meagre, stale, forbidding ways
> Of custom, law and statute, took at once
> The attraction of a country in romance !
> When Heaven seemed the most to assert her rights
> When most intent on making of herself
> A prime enchantress – to assist the work
> Which then was going forward in her name !
> Not favoured spots alone, but the whole Earth
> The beauty wore of promise – that which sets
> (As at some moments might not be unfelt
> Among the bowers of Paradise itself)
> The budding rose above the rose full blown.
> What temper at the prospect did not wake
> To happiness unthought of ?

The revolution in its first appeal beyond the frontiers of France did bring emancipation and something of the message of universal brotherhood.

But it was not long before more permanent strains in the nature of nations began to assert themselves. It soon became apparent that the appeal to universal brotherhood was an even more effective way of expanding the frontiers of France, of realizing the secular objectives of French policy than ever the *ancien régime* had had at its disposal. Soon Belgium and Holland were swallowed up ; Switzerland became the Helvetian Republic ; Genoa the Ligurian Republic, and so on. France was back at her old game, and well on the way to becoming a great military despotism. A European coalition was formed to resist her; Great Britain, a little belatedly, entered the war. Mankind had returned to normal.

The disillusionment on the part of those who had hoped so much was deep and bitter. It has left an undying mark in English literature in the lives and work of Wordsworth, Coleridge, Southey. One can hardly blame them for having hoped too much: they were poets, they were not historians, and they were young. (Older people should have known better what to expect from human beings.) But the experience had a deeply interesting effect on each of them: they all became affected by the historical outlook. Southey became a distinguished historian of the straightforward kind; Coleridge took to metaphysics impregnated with history – from which sprang, among other things, the philosophy of Toryism; Wordsworth turned back for inspiration to Milton and the seventeenth century, and wrote the splendid patriotic sonnets which are a chief legacy in English literature of the long war with Napoleon.

In French historical literature the theme of the essential continuity of French policy through the revolution and under Napoleon with that of the *ancien régime* is the subject of Sorel's masterpiece, *L'Europe et la Révolution Française*.

There is the obvious parallel in our own time with the Russian revolution: the hope, the expectations, the faith; disappointment – the revolution turning back upon itself, eating its own children; the cynicism, complete disillusionment; the return to normal. Russia has not ceased to be Russia for having been through the October Revolution. It may be called communist; but Russian society had a strong communal element before, where English-speaking peoples are individualistic. A good deal besides has been continuous too: the absence of political freedom, the authoritarian régime of the Tsars succeeded by that of Stalin, the important part played by the G.P.U. in succession to the old, and less efficient, secret police. The war with Germany brought out something of the latent patriotism, the invasion revived the feeling for the soil of Holy Russia – the themes of 1812 were uppermost – and even brought about a reconciliation between Stalin and the Church. (The association in Russia was always very close; Stalin was educated by the Church.) And we are witnessing, what will be important for the future of Europe, the return to the long-term objectives of Russian policy.

It may be said that these are lessons the application of which is mainly in the past; what of the future? History shows us that there is no such break between the past and the future. While I write this sentence what was future has already become past. All is continuous. And history, without predicting the future, can offer some useful guide to it. The resumed march of Russia towards her age-long objectives, towards a dominant position in eastern and south-eastern Europe, in the Baltic and the Balkans, towards a Mediterranean outlet, in the Middle and Far East, will occupy important pages in what is to come of twentieth-century history. What should be the shape of Britain's foreign policy in the future? Our best guide is the consistent success of that of the Grand Alliance in the past. In Europe we should construct a system of security in which our interest is at one with that of the great bulk of the whole. Chamberlain in his ignorance of history thought it possible to have an alliance with Nazi Germany; had he realized that only a defensive coalition can check an aggressive over-mighty power, we might have avoided the catastrophe that followed appeasement.

So far as the United States is concerned the conduct of her world policy since the end of the war has merited the leadership of the Western world, for its responsibility, its considerateness of the interests and well-being of others, and for its unexampled generosity. The United States has returned to the direction indicated by Woodrow Wilson, a position corresponding to her world-wide interests and her responsibilities as the greatest of Western powers. The wishful isolationism discernible among some older American historians is totally out of keeping with America's position in the world, and is a disservice to the nation. It goes clean counter to the thesis of this book as to the use of history, and the duty of historians, in forming an educated public opinion, particularly about international affairs.

Such are a few of the directives which a commonsense reading of history would suggest for the future.

But Henry Ford once told us that 'History is all bunk.' There could not be a more symptomatic expression of the superficiality of the modern mechanical mind. Mr Ford really thought in 1927 that he had found the key to the economic problem of our time – with all its maladjustments and strains and conflicts, which had baffled the best intellects of every country – in the simple payment of high wages. In 1929 came the crash of the American boom, and the United States was in for a worse industrial depression than anybody else had had. History, we might say, had caught up with Mr Ford and had found him to be mostly 'bunk'. As if the United States were any exception to the strains and stresses operating in the modern economic system! In so far as we have now arrived at a better understanding of them, we owe it largely to the historically-minded school of economic thought led by Lord Keynes.

It will be obvious then, that so far from any defeatism about history as a subject of study, I have entire confidence in its use. It is a subject that rids you of illusions, one in which you grow up and become adult. The one depressing thought is how little people appear to profit by it. It is rather like what Hegel says: 'The one thing one learns from history is that nobody ever learns anything from history.' And yet they may learn so much. It offers people an inexhaustible store of vicarious experience upon which they may draw, instead of going through it all over again for themselves in ignorance and suffering.

The price to be paid is a very little trouble for a great deal of pleasure. For in addition to the uses of history, of which I have elaborated only one, there are its pleasures.

In the end, we reflect, man's life is very much restricted, confined, in time: a mere three-score and ten years, often not that. If we had only that to go on we should know little indeed. The truth is that without the sense of history human life as we know it would be unthinkable; history is as fundamental to our lives as that. It is only through a knowledge of history that our own brief lives – such a short span of experience – become one with the record of the human race; it is only through history that we know anything of that record and can share in it. The life of the individual breaks its barriers and becomes conterminous with humanity. Bound as our lives are to the tyranny of time, it is through what we know of history that we are delivered from our bonds and escape – into time.

2 The Pleasures of History

So far we have been concerned with the utilitarian aspect of the case. But what about the pleasures of history ? – and they are many. They may turn out to have a use too ; most pleasures have.

Let us begin with what is to me the most obvious, and perhaps the most appealing, pleasures it gives : the way a knowledge of history enriches and fills out our appreciation of the world around us under our eyes. It gives an interest and a meaning to things which perhaps we should not have noticed before, not only villages and towns and buildings, a church, an old house, a bridge, but even the landscape itself.

Half a mile away from my home in Cornwall there is a field, just above the farm of Castle Gotha right on the cliffs, which I had crossed for years before I realized what it was. The name 'Castle Gotha' ought to have aroused my suspicions, given me a clue. You go through the kissing-gates on the road to Trenarren and find yourself in a big enclosure with a magnificent view of the bay and all the inland country to the china-clay uplands. When you pass out through the kissing-gates at the other side you find yourself in a little lane ; it is the remains of the dyke of a prehistoric camp with the broad vallum rising on your left and running away in a semi-circle. Under your feet as you go, you feel the hard track that crosses the field to the headland, where there is a well-marked prehistoric cliff-fortification. In the field on the other side of my house is a tall longstone, one of the finest monoliths in Cornwall, which still has its aura of superstition and fear among the local people of these parts. ('As children we never played in that field,' a woman once told me ; 'they do say that a man was hanged there once – oh, hundreds of years ago.') Further along in the depression where the road goes down to Charlestown there was a number of barrows, demolished when the road was made to the little port.

You begin to see a picture of the life of the primitive folk around this bay in prehistoric times, as it was, say, from 1000 B.C. to A.D. 500: the camp at Castle Gotha which was their 'town', their stronghold; the cliff-camp to which they could retire when danger was greatest – it is a very narrow isthmus across the headland, defended by two considerable vallums or ramparts, and there is a spring of water in the cliff. There is the monolith facing east and west – a most impressive figure it makes in the setting sun – that was the centre of their religious rites, almost certainly involving human sacrifices; there were the barrows where they buried their dead, the chiefs of the tribe.

I am no pre-historian, nor an archaeologist; but when I put together the picture of these remains from prehistoric times, and read a little about those times in Gordon Childe's *Prehistoric Communities of the British Isles*, I confess that the whole thing came alive for me; the life lived around the bay gained a whole dimension: one could see it, the continuous life of those earlier folks, the 'Mediterranean men, my ancestors', going right back to the dim savage shades of unrecorded antiquity.

How much more fascinating, at least to me, are the periods of which we have record.

From my study window I look straight out across the blue waves and white horses of the bay to the headlands on either side of the entrance to Fowey harbour. And I remember the medieval and Elizabethan appearance of that delightful town with all its history. The earlier dedication of the church, to St Finbarrus of Cork, tells us of the town's important trade with Ireland in the Middle Ages; Irish merchants formed a considerable contingent of the early settlers who made the town.

In the Middle Ages Fowey was the most important of Cornish ports; under its leadership they sent forty-seven ships, a larger contribution than any other save London's, to the armada with which Edward III besieged Calais in 1347. In the church, in the Treffry chapel, are the achievements of John Treffry who fought under the Black Prince at Poitiers and took the French royal standard. That chapel is full of their memorials, of the brothers Sir John, William and Thomas, who were well known to Henry VIII and Cromwell, and took an active part on the side of the Reformation in Cornwall. Above the church towers their fine house of Place, which an earlier Treffry lady of the fifteenth century had defended heroically against the French when they burnt the town. That was a reprisal for the depredations of John Mixtow and the merry men of Fowey upon French ships in the Channel – you may read about it in C. L. Kingsford's sedate *Prejudice and Promise in the Fifteenth Century*. When I walk through those vivacious, angular cramped streets I think as I look up at the windows of Place – that decorated stone front overlooking all the town – of another episode in English history : of Philip II's chests of gold, intended for the payment of Alva's troops in the Netherlands in 1569, which were interned for the Queen at Saltash and Fowey, and those very same chests reposing in Mr Treffry's cellars until fetched up to the Tower of London. For want of that cash, Alva's troops mutinied – which gave a breathing-space to the Netherlanders fighting for their liberty ; and it made a turning-point in the relations between England and Spain.

On the other side of the lime-walk from the church is the Ship Inn – the old house of the Rashleighs, not far from the quay where they did business so profitably in the days of Elizabeth. Upstairs you may still see the black oak-panelled best room of John Rashleigh and his wife Alice, with a fine carved mantelpiece supported by caryatids – the impulse of the Italian Renaissance reaching this remote West-country spot ; the date, 1570. They both of them lie quiet enough now in the church across the way ; Alice under her chaste brass beneath the pulpit, her husband in full Elizabethan black gown and white ruff upon his painted tomb. They owned a famous little ship, the *Francis of Fowey*, which made a fortune for them as a privateer in those disturbed days in the Channel and the Bay of Biscay. Their son sailed her up to Plymouth to fight under Drake against the Armada in 1588. The next generation bought land; left Fowey and commerce for the lovely Gribbin peninsula, where they built their home at Menabilly – still looking out to sea. A generation later the civil war descended upon them there; and precisely three hundred years ago this very summer in which I write, the Parliamentarian army under Essex was cooped up in that peninsula by the Royalist army under the King and forced to surrender – but not before they had eaten all Mr Rashleigh's cattle and livestock, 10,000 sheep (so he claimed). From these fields, then open downs, one must have been able to see all the soldiery swarming over that narrow neck of land.

And so one could go on – but I am not writing a history of Fowey. I am merely showing you how the landscape comes alive when you know the history that lies behind it. Nor is it only martial events like sieges and battles, civil wars and the burning of towns, that light it up. There is all the romance and pathos of industry, the mines that were once hives sounding with the activity of hundreds of men, now all closed down, ruined shells of engine-houses, the refuse dumps once more carpeted with green.

> The places that are empty now
> Were once so full of vivid life.

In the near foreground upon the cliffs stands the shell of Appletree mine; the workings went far out under the bay. To the left, where now Campdowns spreads its garment of gorse and withies and ash, was a rich mining district with a number of mines. They all had to close down in the eighteen-seventies and -eighties, and hundreds of men left home to work the mines in South Africa, Montana, Michigan, Australia. Quite near across the cornfield is Charlestown Foundry, the oldest foundry in Cornwall to be working continuously to this day. All this – the nineteenth-century mining development of Cornwall, the pathetic emigration of thousands of Cornish miners all over the world (you will come across one of them portrayed in Stevenson's *Across the Plains*) – is but a part of the story of the Industrial Revolution which looms so formidably in the text-books under that name.

In later years it has been a poignant experience to follow these Cornish folk overseas to their old mining settlements in

such places as the Upper Peninsula of Michigan, very characteristic and delightful Mineral Point in Wisconsin, Grass Valley
in California and ghost-towns like Jerome in Arizona. No doubt
it would be much the same in Canada, South Africa, Australia.
People hardly appreciate the interesting and diverse contributions the Cornish have made through generations to American
life, where there must be more Cornish folk now than at home
in Cornwall. For an example of one distinguished Cornish-
American family, consult *The Penrose Family*.

If this is only one tithe of what comes to mind from looking
out of a window in Cornwall, upon a small and not particularly
significant part of the English scene, you can imagine what richness, what delights there are in walking the streets of a town
like Oxford, or Bristol, or York, or Carlisle, or Edinburgh, or
London. I cannot begin to give you an idea of what it is like to
live in a place like Oxford, there are so many layers of memories
and associations, there is no end to the pleasure of exploring
them. Not that I have set out deliberately to explore them – for
I have made Cornwall my chosen field of investigation ; it is
just that they come to mind and fill every moment with interest
and fascination. When I go down into the quadrangle I think of
the historian Froude turning in at the gate of All Souls from the
traffic of the High and in the quietness meditating upon the Oxford of thirty years before, the Oxford of Newman and the
Tractarians. From my room I can always see the spire of Newman's St Mary's, the University church, which has those other
memories, Cranmer's last withdrawal of his recantation on the
way to the stake, Amy Robsart's burial in the chancel. Or if I
walk in the Meadows there is the civil war that conjures up
scenes in my mind : young Colonel Windebank being shot
against the city wall that is the boundary of Merton College ;
Merton itself the palace of Henrietta Maria ; the King housed in
Christ Church – they made a door through the wall that the
two might visit each other privately. Often on my pedestrian
way to the station, bent prosaically upon catching a train, I
catch sight of the Norman tower of the Castle ; and my mind
goes back to Geoffrey of Monmouth, who was a canon of the
chapel there in the twelfth century, and wrote his work on the

Histories of the Kings of Britain in those remote faraway days. Never was there a book that had a more prodigious influence upon the literature of Europe, save only the Bible; for from it came the flowering of the Arthurian legend in all the languages and arts of western Europe, in French, Italian, German, English, Spanish. Think only in our own language of Malory and Spenser, of Tennyson, Arnold, Swinburne and Hardy, who all go back to that twelfth-century book written somewhere down that forgotten road.

It may be said that Oxford is a special case, as in a way it is. Living there as a boy was an inspiration to one English historian, J. R. Green: he was born there, went to Magdalen College School, grew up in its streets, loving every nook and cranny of the place, and before he ceased to be an undergraduate had written the first of his famous essays, 'Oxford in the Last Century'. It came out as a series of articles in the local paper, the *Oxford Chronicle*. Already it was not a far cry to his famous *Short History of the English People*; such masterpieces have such beginnings.

Every old town is a special case. Many of them have beauty – alas, much damaged not merely by the Teutonic barbarian but by our own barbarians who know nothing either of history or beauty, people who know nothing, see nothing, understand nothing, appreciate nothing. These old towns all have their own character and interest. Think of Norwich, full of churches and the feeling of being a centre still of medieval trade; of Bristol with its finger on the pulses of the sea and all those voyages going out of the port to America, and the monuments of the merchants in the city churches. Or there is Carlisle, with its sombre sense of a border fortress town, the fine West Walks overlooking the flats, the Castle looking out over the Debatable Lands to Scotland; one thinks of Mary, Queen of Scots, viewing from the ramparts the football match between her retinue and the garrison. Or York, with its magnificent sense of space and of being a capital. How many kings have entered the city in triumph or in defeat; there is the tragic figure of the Lord President of the North, Strafford, that haunts the splendid house that once was the abbot's of St Mary's; or a more endearing shade, the whimsical, fantastic man of genius, Laurence Sterne, finding it difficult to stand up to his formidable uncle, treasurer of the Minster. Or there is Edinburgh, the most striking town in these Islands, stretched out along the sharp spine of rock between the Castle and Holyrood – each with its dramatic stories, the little room in the palace where the Scottish lords hacked Rizzio to death in the presence of their Queen ; the more genial shadow on the blind of the quick pen racing across the pages, the unknown 'author of Waverley'. Or there is London. It is difficult for English people to see London from the outside or grasp its character. We take it so much for granted – far too much for granted ; it is the terminus of our journeys, a world, a fate ; there is something inevitable about it. But a distinguished Dane, Rasmussen, who had written a good book on it, says that it has a *stronger* character of its own than any other town in the world. The leading American authority on cities and their culture, Lewis Mumford, has paid it a similar tribute.

When you come to great towns like London or Paris, Vienna or Rome – or Antwerp, Florence, Venice, Constantinople – you reach the plane of historic events on an international scale. Their memories are inexhaustible, of the greatest events and men. For the historical development of cities, their nature and function in civilization, read Lewis Mumford's fine book, *The City in History*.

I have taken you from history in the immediate vicinity to history played on the largest stage of national and international affairs. Let us return to the parish. For here there is not only the pleasure awaiting you when you begin to open your eyes and store your mind, but the pleasure you can pursue across country with much less trouble and expense than following the hounds.

Walking is the favourite sport of 'the good and the wise'. This is not the place to sing its praises in and for itself ; that has been done by Leslie Stephen and Meredith, by R. L. Stevenson and G. M. Trevelyan, best of all by Hazlitt. I want to make a point that is not made by any of them : walking is the way to see the country. But what an agreeable addition it is to the pleasure of walking to have some interesting object in view : to saunter through an old village, linger in the church over the monuments and things of beauty, eat your sandwiches by a ford that had its part in the Wars of the Roses, trespass as far as you can through the park to get a good view of the old mansion, still Tudor in its main lines, though you mark with interest the seventeenth- and eighteenth-century additions – calling up in the mind the continuous life of the family there through all the changes of the Henries, Edwards, Elizabeth, the Georges. Later in the afternoon you rest at a spot where you can look down upon the outlines of a Roman villa in the valley below, or you step aside to view a stone circle – perhaps the Rollright stones in the northern Cotswolds which Shakespeare must often have looked at with observant eye. You may have tea in an old inn, in the porch of which (if it is Devon) the Cavalier poet Sidney Godolphin died, or where (if it is Oxfordshire) John Hampden lingered his last days.

The country is infinitely rich in memories, and old buildings, country houses or yeomen's farms, barns, or bridges or byres. Every parish has its church, usually an old one, with its memorials left behind by the tides and currents of life that have flowed through it. Any walk you choose to take can have a fascination for a cultivated mind. One would not be uncultivated for any-thing. For that way lies infinite boredom and dreariness of spirit. The truest thing – and the most useful – that ever Dean Inge said was that 'the true intellectual is never bored'. And what a strength that is, when one thinks of it. A friend of mine, the Cornish antiquary and historian, Charles Henderson, had the habit from his schooldays of walking or taking a bus or train to some particular parish and then settling down upon it for the day, traversing it, following its boundaries, looking up everything of interest in it, camp or stone-circle, holy-well or chapel, villages and farms. Often it meant several visits, return-ing to the same parish. It was that that filled out and made real and concrete his remarkable knowledge of documents and deeds relating to the past. In this way he came to know not only every parish and church in Cornwall, but almost every farm and field. This is the way that historians are made. It could not be better put than by R. H. Tawney when he tells us that what economic history needs at present is not more documents but a pair of sturdy boots.

In America a car is indispensable, if only to transport you to the points at which excursions may begin. It is still best to traverse a historic city like Philadelphia on foot, starting with the Swedish church at the beginning, going on to a fine Georgian monument like Christ Church, thence to Carpenters' Hall, the old Market and so to the heart of things with Independence Hall. For the historic houses along the Schuylkill, in the suburbs and further out – beautiful Andalusia of the Biddles, the Highlands, or Graeme Park – a car is necessary. The book to take, if possible, is Howard D. Eberlein's *Philadelphia: Portrait of a Colonial City*.

Or there are the pleasures of exploring such unspoiled places as exquisite Newcastle, Delaware, or Newburyport and Salem, Massachusetts. I mention these as the first to come to mind. Then a flood of such places comes back to memory : the Spanish Missions of California, the strong idiosyncrasy of New Orleans, or of Charleston or Savannah, the poignant civil war memories of the rival capitals, Richmond and Washington, of the great valley of Virginia ; the beauty of Charlottesville, Monticello and Mount Vernon ; the silent eloquence of the site of Jamestown ; the battlefields of Valley Forge, Brandywine and Gettysburg.

The point is that everywhere there is something to awaken the historic imagination and satisfy the sense of beauty.

Then there is reading. Perhaps I should have dealt with this first, since most people think of history in terms of books to read. But I wanted to drive home that the things we see around us, a town or village, a church, a harbour or bit of wall, even a field or a stretch of landscape, are all documents for history as much as a charter or land-book, a title-deed, a letter or a will. Often the two relate to each other, the land to the title-deed, the house and its furnishings to the will, the landscape to the letter. They illuminate each other. The point about the written evidences is that they are usually more precise ; of their nature they define what is in question ; often they will give one the date, or the place of the event in the sequence of the story.

There is a famous and too-much discussed dictum of Croce's,

'All history is contemporary history.' I do not think there is more in it than this, that we know the past only through the evidences that survive, directly or indirectly, into the present and are in our minds now, as with any other knowledge. Not a particularly valuable thought. Of course there is more implied in it than that, and some of what is implied is very debatable; we may be able to turn to it later. This approach to history is sound in so far as it comes to this, in common-sense terms : that the past is not something dead, shut away like a series of damp catacombs, which you enter by a difficult and uncongenial mode of ingress (in other words, an examination-course on unappetizing textbooks) – it is alive and all about one. History is about life and has the appeal of life itself ; the feeling for history is a nostalgia for life, subtly transmuted. That is the answer to the question of one of the most academic, and at the same time poetic, of present-day historians, F. M. Powicke :

Shepherds have kept their sheep in all ages: why am I stirred so deeply because I can trace the very sheep-walks of the monks of Furness? Why is there a remote, yet strangely familiar, music about the names of places – Beverley, Gainsborough, Thrapston, Tewkesbury – a music in which it is impossible to distinguish the call of authentic English speech from the echoes of a hundred insistent associations? ... It is the sense of the past that comes to us from the Middle Ages as it came to the young American in Henry James's story, as he wandered about his eighteenth-century house in London – 'the sense of a conscious past, recognizing no less than recognizable'. The place was a museum, 'but a museum of held reverberations'. So long as we are conscious of these 'held reverberations', history will continue to entice us. So long as their mystery endures, and it will always endure, the past will continue to escape us.

That opens up another and subtler question, to which we shall return.

Because history is vibrant with life, pulsates with it – Carlyle said that it was the essence of innumerable biographies – reading biographies is a good way of beginning to read history. Perhaps it is the best of all for beginners. Everybody is interested in personality ; everybody loves a story – or he is a very

dull dog who does not. That makes me very much in favour of
the biographical approach, especially with children, in teaching
history in schools. Everybody knows, or should know, that the
important thing is to arouse their interest. It applies not only
to children but to all of us. It is merely sound psychology that
we find it easier to pick up knowledge that interests us than
what doesn't interest us. I suffer from what the Church calls a
state of invincible ignorance about anything mechanical, because my interest is not engaged. But the life of a human being,
particularly an exciting one, fascinates me ; and the great figures
of history have all had exciting lives. There is no end to the
interest in the extraordinary personalities of people like Queen
Elizabeth I, Cromwell, Nelson, Swift, William the Silent, Riche-
lieu, Benjamin Franklin, Lincoln, the Roosevelts, Winston
Churchill.

There is one obvious danger in reading history from biographies : you may get a one-sided view of the subject. The
remedy for this is to read the lives of men on both sides. As
Trevelyan says :

The lives of rival statesmen, warriors and thinkers provided they
are good books, are often the quickest route to the several points
of view that composed the life of an epoch. *Ceteris paribus*, a
single biography is more likely to mislead than a history of the
period, but several biographies are often more deeply instructive
than a single history.

I have only scratched the surface of the interest in human
personality that is excited, and satisfied, by historical biography.
In truth, in its full depth and in the round, the appeal is the same
as that of characters in a novel, of characters in a great novel.
There is the conflict of characters, the mutual likes and dislikes,
the loves and hatreds ; the conflicts within one person, the ir-
rationalities, the divided loyalties ; there is the subtle complexity
of motive ; the strange patterns that our lives fall into, the
drama and tragedy of so many of them upon the public scene.
The people in Tolstoy's *War and Peace* have the same appeal as
the actual people in history. In historical writing there is always
and at every point the limitation of truth; but that is an advantage as much as a limitation. Tolstoy was not confined to telling

the truth about Napoleon; the result is that we get a very unfair and biased account of him. Napoleon was a far more remarkable man, in spite of his obvious defects, than Tolstoy
gives us any idea of. On the other hand, if we take a character
like Turgenev's Bazarov in *Fathers and Children*, he is just like
a portrait out of Herzen's *Memoirs*, just as authentic and convincing.

Then there is the pleasure, and the importance, of the story
in itself. It is here, perhaps, that contemporary historians are
weakest. They are not entirely to be blamed for it; for it is
partly due to the enormous increase in the amount of subject-
matter – economic, social, archaeological, what not – to be
subsumed in a modern history. The extension of the range of
history is all to the good; and as and when the absorption of
the new material advances, the ability of contemporary historians to cope with it improves, one may expect the art of narrative to return to its central position in historical writing. For
after all, the very word 'history', the fact that it is cognate
with 'story', shows you that narrative is the backbone of history.

Its appeal, and the pleasure of it, are elemental. It is as primitive and fundamental in a society as that of the epic, of the
Iliad and *Odyssey*, or of the Icelandic sagas. It is the *story* that
holds our attention in childhood, as in the childhood of peoples.
The concern with truth, the delimitation of fact from fiction – in
short, the development of historical writing – is a later, more
sophisticated stage. Thucydides is many centuries later than
Homer; Gibbon centuries later than Chaucer. All the same it is
essentially the story in both Thucydides and Gibbon that grips
the mind: it marches on remorselessly like a tragedy to its inevitable end, like Meredith's 'army of unalterable law', or like
the sea across the bay under my eyes as I write.

But was it inevitable, unalterable? Ah, there begin the subtle
and exciting *intellectual* issues of history. For the present we
will confine ourselves to the remark that the appeal of the story
is like that of *Gulliver's Travels*, one that grows with you as
you grow in mind, ripens with your own experience of life,
deepens and comes to have much more meaning for you as you

achieve maturity. In childhood it may have the same appeal as a fairy-story or a tale of adventure ; in later life it may come to have a philosophical meaning. Therein lies a large part of the satisfaction in historical study : it is a study that grows with you, a subject that was capable of interesting you as a child does not fail to reward you, but has an even deeper interest for the grown man.

Nearly all the great historians have been masters of narration. As we have seen, it was easier for them than for us with the vast masses of material, and of such different kinds, for us to absorb into our books. All the same, it was never easy ; it demanded art, craftsmanship, long labour. Gibbon took years learning to write – and with what results ! In our time when there are so many people writing who are not artists, and so many writing history who take far more trouble searching for new material than composing what they find, nothing like enough attention is paid to composition, arrangement, style. That makes inferior writers more difficult to read. 'But easy writing's vile hard reading,' said Sheridan. No such difficulty with Macaulay, who took infinite pains with his writing. 'In arrangement,' Trevelyan says, 'that is to say in the planning of the book, in the way subject leads on to subject and paragraph to paragraph, Macaulay's *History* has no equal and ought to be carefully studied by everyone who intends to write a narrative history.'

Hence it is that historians are among the great writers of most ages which have achieved maturity and sophistication – for reflection upon the past is a sign of maturity, and there is something sophisticated in the desire to tell only the truth, that essential and self-willed limitation upon the historian. Thucydides was among the greatest of Greek writers in antiquity, and Herodotus, the founder of a different tradition, the father of both social history and anthropology, comes but little behind him. Livy and Tacitus are among the great Roman writers, as Commines and Froissart are among those of medieval France, or Machiavelli and Guicciardini of Renaissance Italy. Though we have no Shakespeare or Milton among English historians, it is not altogether inappropriate to compare Clarendon, who stands at the head of the English tradition of historical writing, to Milton. There is the same magnificent architectonic sense, the marshalling of experience, the same deep undercurrent of emotion. And though *Paradise Lost* is great poetry, there is perhaps more romantic feeling in Clarendon. Gibbon and Hume are among the leading writers of their age ; Carlyle, Macaulay, Froude of theirs. And lesser historians even, J. R. Green, Creighton, Seeley, Acton, are distinguished men of letters. Parkman and Prescott, Motley, and Henry Adams are among the most eminent writers of New England. All these historians, and many more, offer you the delights of literature.

There is another aspect of this question of the relations between history and literature. Historians not only contribute directly to literature, but a knowledge of history enters in varying degrees into the appreciation of literature. Perhaps it enters least into the appreciation of pure poetry or drama, and most into that of political literature where the subject-matter is bound up with history. Because the English have long been a politically conscious people they have a rich and varied political literature, from Sir Thomas More and Tyndale to Bacon and Hooker and Ralegh ; Milton and Hobbes and Locke ; Swift and Burke ; Hazlitt, Carlyle, John Stuart Mill.

Similarly in America, where the political writings of Franklin and John Dickinson, of John Adams and Jefferson, Hamilton, Madison and Monroe – that remarkable outpouring of talent at the time of the revolution, that has left permanent memorials in *The Federalist* and elsewhere – form part of the classic tradition of American literature. In much of what these men wrote it is essential to know the history to know what they are talking about, what are the issues being discussed.

It is not only in this realm of literature that a knowledge of history is helpful or even indispensable, it may be with regard to novels – the novels of Scott and Disraeli, for example, or for that matter of Stendhal and Balzac, or some of the novels of Flaubert, Tolstoy, Turgenev. Nor does it end here. It may be of immense value in enabling you to understand, and derive a fuller pleasure from, the drama – the plays of Shakespeare, or of the Restoration theatre, of Dryden and Congreve, Goldsmith and Sheridan. The same holds good of a great deal of poetry, of Milton and Dryden, Wordsworth, Scott and Byron. *The Prelude* is possibly the greatest work of literature to owe its impulse to the French revolution, and it is not properly understandable without knowing something of Wordsworth's relation to that universal event. But even works of a more remote, a more purely poetic character, like Spenser's *Faerie Queene*, or Tennyson's *Idylls of the King*, are illuminated for us, and our pleasure heightened, by a knowledge of the history that has gone into them and the contemporary background which they in part express. And we may savour something of the latter even in the purest lyric poetry – say Christina Rossetti's *Goblin Market*. Of course the aesthetic reaction to a work of art comes first in the case of literature – that should go without saying ; but the historic appreciation in no way conflicts with it – it complements it and fills it out.

Reading history, then, opens out fresh fields, illimitable beckoning horizons to the imagination. The pleasure of it, as Macaulay says : 'is analogous, in many respects, to that produced by foreign travel. The student, like the tourist, is transported into a new state of society. He sees new fashions. He hears new modes of expression. His mind is enlarged by contemplating the wide diversities of laws, of morals and of manners. But men may travel far, and return with minds so contracted as if they had never stirred from their own market towns.' And so Macaulay makes his plan for sinking shafts deep into society and writing the whole life, as far as possible, of a people, not resting content with a lifeless skeleton of the names and dates of battles and genealogies of royal houses.

He who would understand these rightly must not confine his observations to palaces and solemn days. He must see ordinary men as they appear in their ordinary business and in their ordinary pleasures. He must mingle in the crowds of the exchange and the coffee-house. He must obtain admittance to the convivial table and the domestic hearth. He must bear with vulgar expressions. He must not shrink from exploring even the retreats of misery. He who wishes to understand the condition of mankind in former ages must proceed on the same principle.

Such was Macaulay's programme in the brilliant essay on history which he wrote as a young man for the *Edinburgh Review*. In maturity he carried out his precepts in the famous third chapter of his *History*, on the state of society in the age, which helped to account for the enthusiasm with which the book was received. Macaulay himself modestly declared, 'I shall not be satisfied unless I produce something which shall for a few days supersede the last fashionable novel on the tables of young ladies.' He succeeded in producing a book that has held the attention of the English-speaking world undiminished for the last century.

In the end, we see history as a compound of fact and imagination, of the imagination picturing the facts, lapping round them, like sea round the rocks upon the coast. The province of the intellect is to interpret the facts, reduce them to order, extract their significance. We shall come to that later. But, as Trevelyan says:

> At bottom the appeal of history is imaginative. Our imagination craves to behold our ancestors as they really were, going about their daily business and their daily pleasure.... It is the detailed study of history that makes us feel that the past was as real as the present.... It is only by study that we can see our fore-runners remote and recent, in their habits as they lived, intent each on the business of a long-vanished day, riding out to do homage or to poll a vote; to seize a neighbour's manor house and carry off his ward, or to leave cards on ladies in crinolines.... Truth is the criterion of historical study; but its impelling motive is poetic.

All the best historians have felt this; though not all of them have been equally able, or perhaps even wished, to express it. The fact is that the experience at the heart of our feeling for history is closer to poetry than is generally realized; in truth, I think it is in essence the same. The moment of illumination which Wordsworth expressed in 'Tintern Abbey', in the ode on 'Intimations of Immortality', and again and again in *The Prelude*, is not essentially different from the moment of evocation and perception at the core of the historian's experience. The historians have given expression to it, but I know that many people who are not historians share it and recognize the experience. Froude has captured it in a justly famous passage of his *History* :

For, indeed, a change was coming upon the world, the meaning and direction of which even still is hidden from us, a change from era to era. The paths trodden by the footsteps of ages were broken up; old things were passing away, and the faith and the life of ten centuries were dissolving like a dream. Chivalry was dying: the abbey and the castle were soon together to crumble into ruins; and all the forms, desires, beliefs, convictions of the old world were passing away, never to return. A new continent had risen up beyond the western sea. The floor of heaven, inlaid with stars, had sunk back into an infinite abyss of immeasurable space; and the firm earth itself, unfixed from its foundations, was seen to be but a small atom in the awful vastness of the universe. In the fabric of habit in which they had so laboriously built for them-selves, mankind were to remain no longer.

And now it is all gone -- like an unsubstantial pageant faded; and between us and the old English there lies a gulf of mystery which the prose of the historian will never adequately bridge. They cannot come to us, and our imagination can but feebly penetrate to them. Only among the aisles of our cathedrals, only as we gaze upon their silent figures sleeping on their tombs, some faint conceptions float before us of what those men were when they were alive; and perhaps in the sound of church bells, that peculiar creation of medieval age, which falls upon the ear like the echo of a vanished world.

At any moment the experience may take us unawares, when something recalls the past ; not necessarily the conscious prose of the great historian ; it may be a fifteenth-century merchant of the Staple away at Calais, writing to his girl-bride in Oxford-shire :

Be a good eater of your meat alway, that ye may wax and grow fat to be a woman ... and greet well my horse and pray him to give you four of his years to help you withal. And I will at my coming home give him four of my years and four horse-loaves to make amends. Tell him that I prayed him so.... And Almighty Jesu make you a good woman and send you alway many good years and long to live in health and virtue to his pleasure. Written at Calais the first of June, when every man was gone to his dinner, and the clock smote noon and all our household cried after me and bade me come down. 'Come down to dinner at once!' And what answer I gave to them ye know of old.

One's heart stands still ; it is one of those moments when time falls away from us ; our feeling for that man who has been dead for centuries is the feeling for ourselves, the sense of our own life slipping away even as his.

The love of history is an expression – not the less beautiful, but the more poignant, for being transmuted, indirect – of the love of life.

3 What History is About

There are two ways of thinking of history. There is, first, history regarded as a way of looking at other things, really the temporal aspect of anything, from the universe to the pen-nib with which I am writing. Everything has its history. There is the history of the universe, if only we knew it – and we know something of it, if we do not know much. Nor is the contrast so great, when you think of it, between the universe and the pen-nib. A mere pen-nib has quite a considerable history. There is, to begin with, what has been written with it, and that might be something quite important. After all it was probably only one quill-pen or a couple that wrote *Hamlet*. Whatever has been written with the pen-nib is part of its history. In addition to that there is the history of its manufacture ; this particular nib is a 'Relief' nib, No. 314, made by R. Esterbrook and Company in England. Behind this nib there is the whole process of manufacture ; I do not know the processes, but one could learn them and thus acquire an introduction to the history of the Industrial Revolution. Beyond that there are the various metals that have gone into the making of the nib : iron, tin, copper, let us say ; the iron may have come from Sweden, the copper from Spain, the tin from Malaya. Anyhow, one sees that the history of a mere pen-nib involves one in the processes of industry, in a knowledge of geography and of geology, and there is no knowing what else may be relevant. In fact a pen-nib implies the universe, and the story of it implies the story of the universe.

We may regard this way of looking at it – history as the time-aspect of all things : a pen-nib, the universe, the field before me as I write, a person (perhaps you who are reading me now), an institution – the Church you belong to, or the country to which we belong – as a relative conception of history.

There is, secondly, what we may call a substantive conception of history, what is usually meant by it, history proper as a subject of study in itself.

What is history, as a subject in itself, about then?

Sir Charles Firth gives us something to begin on:

History is not easy to define; but to me it seems the record of the life of societies of men, of the changes which those societies have gone through, of the ideas which have determined the actions of those societies, and of the material conditions which have helped or hindered their development.

That gives us a practical working definition, not necessarily exhaustive, but at any rate central to the subject. Notice that it is much wider than you might expect from an old-fashioned nineteenth-century historian. Firth was an academic historian of the purest water. He made no concessions whatever to the reader, or to anybody else. He had the strictest standards of scholarship; he had a searching critical sense, a keen edge to his intellect. This, added to a certain defect in his emotional nature, a North-country grittiness of mind, inhibited him as a writer. He was a devotee of the impersonal in history – as if you can cease being yourself, however impersonal you may try to be! The result was that he was the finest example of the historical scholar of his time, rather than the finest historian. He was in truth an historians' historian, in the way that some poets, like Spenser for example, are peculiarly the choice of their fellows, or Flaubert a novelists' novelist. Firth exemplified in himself his own catholic principle of scholarship; of his own period, the seventeenth century, no one has ever known more. He knew more than Macaulay; and this extraordinary detailed knowledge extended forward to include a great deal of the eighteenth century and backward to include much of the sixteenth. He set himself to know all that there was to be known about his period, not only the documents in print and in manuscript, but the literature.

Though Firth was the type of the academic historian, in fact he was altogether more catholic and comprehensive than Marxist writers who criticize the type without being able to provide a better example. His own writings covered many aspects of his period; he contributed not to one only but to several fields of history. The biggest of his books, his continuation of Gardiner's history, *The Last Years of the Protectorate*, belongs to political history. *The House of Lords during the Civil War* is an important contribution to constitutional history. His book *Cromwell's Army* is a standard work in military history, his life of Oliver Cromwell the most authoritative biography. There are many essays, studies and editions of works, which are contributions not only to the history of literature but to social history. And though he did not write specifically on economic history, an essay like his 'London in the Civil War' attests his appreciation of the importance of the economic factor.

Firth's predecessor at Oxford, York Powell, had a similarly wide conception of what history should be, even if he did not carry it out in his own exiguous writing.

It deals with the condition of masses of mankind living in a social state. It seeks to discover the laws that govern these conditions and bring about changes we call Progress and Decay, and Development and Degeneracy – to understand the process that gradually or suddenly make up or break up those political and economic agglomerations we call States – to find out the circumstances affecting the various tendencies that show their power at different times.

These wide and sympathetic views were developed perhaps in conscious reaction to the limitation of history to political history. The apostle of this view was Seeley, who was in the habit of insisting to his pupils that 'the history of the Staffordshire Potteries was *not* history'. He was interested only in the life of the state, and the conflicts of power between states : he was much influenced by German models. Not being a brilliant writer himself, he did not hold with history as literature. Trevelyan enters a protest at having been solemnly instructed as an undergraduate at Cambridge 'by the author of *Ecce Homo* that Macaulay and Carlyle did not know what they were writing about, and that "literary history" was a thing of naught'. The reaction in Trevelyan's case has done nothing but good ; it stimulated him to achieve a body of work that is not only history but literature.

History is, then, essentially the record of the life of men in societies in their geographical and physical environment. Their social and cultural environment arises from the interaction of the one with the other, the society and its geographical conditions.

That gives one the groundwork of history; it is not the background, it is the story itself, the story of human society, or the stories of human societies. Upon that groundwork all the variety and detail of history arise. The individual is a social product, the child of given parents in a certain condition of life, a member of a particular family with its characteristics; he belongs to a particular class of society, is moulded and made by school and friends and church and university. The converse is also true: society is made up of individuals, and history is made up of millions of particular events and instances. Some schools of thought emphasize the one, other schools emphasize the other. To my mind there is no real conflict between mass and the individual in the proper understanding of history. They are complementary to each other. The mass is more important in determining the long-term course of events; understanding the mass-movements of society is more important to *understanding* history. The individual is more important in the realm of values; it is his standards that evaluate those movements. It is the life of the individual that is the ultimate thing in human experience. We may say that the importance of the one is intellectual and scientific, of the other spiritual and aesthetic. And it depends on what angle you are tackling the subject from, which approach is more appropriate and should be given more prominence.

We have come to conceive of history as the history of society *as a whole*. Neither Firth nor York Powell carried out his precept; the latter never tried to. One can well understand why – because of the innate difficulty of the task. I appreciate those difficulties, having attempted an example of such a total history in my *Tudor Cornwall*, and later with *The England of Elizabeth*. To portray a whole society in all its aspects, its geographical environment, its economic foundation, the land system and its industries, the governmental and administrative system, the social structure, the political events, the social, religious and cultural life – it is probable that it can only be done at all fully for a small society and in miniature. If the scale becomes much enlarged it becomes almost impossible to do it and to retain the concrete, pictorial treatment; the work may have to become a work of synthesis and lose vivid individuality. Yet the impulse towards this kind of total history – giving an account of a society in all its aspects – is unmistakable in contemporary writing. The idea behind the new Oxford History of England reflects it, though a series of text-books can hardly exemplify. The first volume of Halévy's *History of the English People in the Nineteenth Century*, devoted to describing the condition of England in 1815, affords a better example with a larger canvas. With Trevelyan's *England in the Age of Queen Anne* it has produced a masterpiece.

*

Having declared my sympathy with the movement for total history, I return to the case of political history. Since we agree that it is the life of the whole society that we are portraying, with its movements and conflicts, mistakes and achievements, its groups and individual figures, it is clear that politics has a central place; for it is upon the plane of politics that all these things are projected and expressed. Politics consists of the public behaviour of men in the mass; it is the society's sphere of action. It is of central importance in the life of a society. And similarly political history must always be the backbone of history. The greatest histories – Thucydides, Gibbon, Macaulay – are all political histories. In the contemporary reaction against a too narrow, political interpretation there is some danger of this being forgotten. That is why I welcome these words of Sir George Clark:

I will even venture to say that we ought still to treat the life of each community in each period as a whole. Many historians are indeed now dissatisfied with the old way of taking political and constitutional history as the central thread through the diversity.

Economic history has vindicated its right to a high place; social history puts forward a strong claim. But it is in public institutions that men express their will to control events, and therefore it seems to me that historians will go wrong if they try to resolve political and constitutional history into other elements, just as our practical men will go wrong if they follow the current fashion of treating 'cultural' interests and activities as if they could be altogether separated from the affairs of states. The history of institutions must be in some sense central.

This last sentence gives us a clue to some further definitions. Political and constitutional history are very close together; political history is the record of the public events in the life of the society, constitutional history gives you the story of its institutions, the political and administrative framework that keeps the society together and enables it to work. Some people make a further distinction between constitutional and administrative history, but one need not trouble about it, for they are indeed the same thing. It happens that in the nineteenth century, owing to the political changes that were taking place, an immense stimulus was given to the study of constitutional history. Two foremost historians were specialists in this field: Stubbs, who wrote a famous *Constitutional History of England*, and Maitland. The generation after them, led by Tout, tended to concentrate on the lesser institutions, filling up the gaps and reinterpreting some of the evidence. So that one may say without unfairness that administrative history is a lesser, and apt to be a less interesting, kind of constitutional history.

Among American constitutional historians perhaps the most eminent is C. H. McIlwain, a philosophic spirit among scholars ; and we may cite the work of G. B. Adams and J. F. Baldwin, for example, on English institutions. On Norman institutions there is the lasting work of the distinguished medievalist, C. H. Haskins, inspiration to many others in those studies. On the constitutional issues involved in the American revolution we may read the eleventh volume of Lawrence H. Gipson's monumental *History of the First British Empire*. Of a younger generation there is the work of Merrill Jensen and E. S. Morgan on the constitutional conflict leading to the revolution.

Since political history is the record of public events, the lives of the leading men who took part in them, often made them, offer a good way of studying it; a way not only attractive in itself, but more appropriate to the subject than perhaps in any other department of history. And naturally the lives of those at the centre of events, those most concerned in directing them, will be of most value and usually the most revealing. A biography of Lenin should be a useful introduction to the history of the Russian revolution; a life of Cromwell to our own seventeenth-century civil war and revolution. From such biographies as Pollard's *Henry VIII* and *Wolsey*, Neale's *Queen Elizabeth*, one may learn a good deal of the political history of the Tudor period. From such detailed 'official' biographies – which means biographies authorized by the representatives of the subject and based upon his personal papers – as Morley's *Gladstone* and Monypenny and Buckle's *Disraeli*, one learns even more about the politics of the nineteenth century.

Constitutional history is much more impersonal; and though it involves the lives of leading men, and much light may be thrown upon it by their biographies, the biographical approach is not the appropriate one. Its subject is the history of institutions; an institution has a life and an interest of its own. I suppose it may be compared to the history of a species or a family in natural science; and those who like that kind of thing are apt to like it very much. But there is one word of warning here. The constitutional historians of the nineteenth century, Hallam, Cornewall Lewis, Erskine May, Stubbs, Maitland, were very much in touch with life and the kind of affairs they were writing about – public affairs and constitutional issues; Cornewall Lewis was a Cabinet Minister with experience of many offices, Erskine May was Clerk of the House of Commons, Stubbs was a bishop, and even Maitland – purest of scholars – intended a political career, which ill-health rendered impossible. And therefore their books have the feeling for public affairs in them, the sense of institutions and their way of working. Too much of constitutional history that is being written nowadays is by people out of touch with affairs, the denizens of libraries rather than of cabinets. They are apt to make the institution an end in itself, and their account of it too far removed from life – sometimes indeed, not to make any bones about it, quite dead and pickled. Now that is very different from Hallam's *Constitutional History*, which is filled with the sense of the living issues of the day ; or from Stubbs, even though he got no further than the Middle Ages in his three volumes ; Stubbs wrote from a large fund of common sense and experience of life, with sturdy vitality and a fine sweep. Even Maitland, who was the ideal of the specialist researcher, was full of life and brilliance ; he was a man of genius and his investigations, the new trails he hit upon, often have the excitement of detective stories to the historian.

Maitland brings us to that fascinating borderland between constitutional history and law – he was trained as a lawyer – and economic history. These studies are close together and throw light on each other, especially in the Middle Ages ; for so much of medieval economic history comes out of legal documents : much material for its agrarian history, for instance, is to be found in manorial records.

How are we to define economic history? Still more, how are we to distinguish it from social history?

A rough-and-ready working distinction can be made by saying that economic history tells you how a society produces its livelihood, social history how it consumes it. Economic history is concerned with the ways and means by which a society gains its subsistence, its land system and methods of agriculture, its industries, trades, businesses, its financial institutions, communications, conditions of labour and its modes of organization and so on.

It is perhaps here that most new ground has been broken in recent decades. Just as the political progressiveness of the nineteenth century was reflected in an increasing interest in constitutional history, so the consciousness of the Industrial Revolution led to a considerable expansion in economic history. The phrase 'the Industrial Revolution' was popularized by Arnold Toynbee's book in the eighteen-eighties. Some of the most interesting of contemporary work is being done in this field, and some of the best of recent historians are economic historians. There was R. H. Tawney, who wrote like an angel – or an Old Testament prophet; Sir George Clark, who writes like an admirable eighteenth-century man of sense; Eileen Power, who wrote like the woman of wit and elegance she was; and there was C. R. Fay – the imp of inspiration that Kipling speaks of in his autobiography sat on the end of his pen. Even more fruitful is the way in which the appreciation of the importance of economic factors has come into the field of vision of historians in general.

'Economic history, the history of man's economic activity,' Sir William Ashley tells us, 'is the history of the utilisation by man of his environment, to obtain therefrom subsistence and the satisfaction of those material wants which are bound up with subsistence. But his activity in this direction, from the very dawn of history, has never been entirely individualistic ; never altogether the operation of absolutely isolated individuals. Some form of association has always been in existence, it would appear, since man became man ; and this has involved some sort, however rudimentary, of distribution of functions – some form, in short, of organisation.' Having said that, Ashley proceeded to write a short book, *The Economic Organisation of England*, which is one of the most illuminating books to be read on the subject.

There is also the variety of economic history in itself, to which Sir George Clark draws attention.

There is, for instance, the history of technology, of tools and machines, of the chemical and other processes of production and transport.... It is a fundamental principle of the evolution of industry that a change of tools or machines brings with it a change of business organisation and of the human relationships which that dictates. Yet in finding out what the development of industrial technique has been, we must go far from the beaten path of historical studies. We must see the material evidence preserved for us in museums, and we must do archaeological field-work in the often deserted and almost forgotten mills or forges of earlier centuries. We must visit modern mines, factories, workshops, farms. We must gather information and ideas from engineers, from chemists, from geologists. For a long time the history of technology has had a life of it own ...

He goes on to discuss the newest fashions for 'business history', which means

sometimes the history of separate firms or businesses, sometimes the history of business in a somewhat wider sense, of business method and organisation.... There are business histories in the heroic or epic manner, of which the theme is the rise of the good man to riches. Others, such as the history of one of our great amalgamated banks, are largely genealogical, and provide useful information on the composition of the business classes in the last three hundred years.

It is obvious what a new field of work is opening up here. We have been given the standard history of the Bank of England by Sir John Clapham ; or there is E. T. MacDermot's fine history of the Great Western Railway. One derives a more human approach in such a book as Miss Sutherland's *An Eighteenth Century Merchant*; or in Richard Pares's *A West India Fortune*.

Indeed the biographical approach offers as many potentialities in the field of economic history as any other, and may well prove the most promising to the general reader. For the writer it is more difficult ; for he has to be skilled, or at least knowledgeable, on the technical side, as well as to present the personality of the subject ; and these two capacities are not often combined. One will often enough come across a biography of a technician – Dickinson and Titley's life of Trevithick is a case in point – which is adequate on the technical side, but jejune on the personal. One needs to combine the two, in the way that C. R. Fay does in his *Great Britain from Adam Smith to the Present Day* or his *English Economic History*. In the latter he has an interesting chapter on 'Desiderata of Industrial Biography'. (It would be a good idea if scholars set themselves to fill these gaps – there are some rewarding subjects.) He analyses the various kinds of such biographies, those written from family piety, those written by the professional biographer who has no other profession than writing biographies – an unhappy type of book, fortunately in decline – those written by the technical expert and those by the professional historian. He gives us an example from each of the last two classes: Sir Alexander Gibb's *The Story of Telford* and T. S. Ashton's *An Eighteenth Century Industrialist, Peter Stubbs of Warrington*. He recommends these as 'biographies which on any test are first-class' and from which 'we may see the ground which a single biography can cover and how it weaves into the pattern of economic history'.

And what wonderful figures and careers there are, full of energy, genius, achievements – sometimes of pathos, often of excitement and romance – in the lives of these inventors, bridge-builders, road-makers, engineers, capitalists. Kipling had the sense of the excitement and creativeness of their lives. What a wealth of great men of this kind there are in English history alone: Robert Hooke and Newcomen, Coke of Holkham, Brindley, the Duke of Bridgwater, Josiah Wedgwood, Arkwright, Boulton and Watt and Murdoch, the Stephensons, Hudson the Railway King, Telford, McAdam, Rennie, the Brunels, Cecil Rhodes and Lord Nuffield, Sir Charles Parsons, the inventors of Spitfires and Hurricanes, radar and jet aircraft. There is no limit to the fascination of these men and women and their lives and works, and no reason why anything should ever be dull.

*

Trevelyan defines social history for us as

the daily life of the inhabitants of the land in past ages: this includes the human as well as the economic relation of different classes to one another, the character of family and household life, the conditions of labour and of leisure, the attitude of man to nature, the culture of each age as it arose out of these general conditions of life, and took ever-changing forms in religion, literature and music, architecture, learning and thought.

And he says roundly: 'Without social history, economic history is barren and political history is unintelligible.' This is an emphasis in the right direction; coming from the most exemplary political historian of our day, it shows how strong a set there is towards a social conception of history. One can understand what it is in our time that impels us towards it, a time when the foundations of civilization have been threatened, all canons of social behaviour questioned, and society itself over large areas on the brink of dissolution. The problems of society are in the forefront of any twentieth-century mind, as those of political organization were in the nineteenth-century. Consciousness of society, with its problems, disturbing and profound, is precipitated into the forefront of our minds. One agreeable by-product is a deepening of our sense of history, and the erection of what used to be thought merely decorative into a distinct and fruitful category of its own.

Social history has its own difficulties, though charming to read: its very continuity, the slowness and subtlety of its changes. Trevelyan tells us what they are:

Social change moves like an underground river, obeying its own laws or those of economic change, rather than following the direction of political happenings that move on the surface of life. Politics are the outcome rather than the cause of social change. A new King, a new Prime Minister, a new Parliament, often marks a new epoch in politics, but seldom in the life of a people. How then is the tale to be told? Into what periods shall social history be divided up? As we look back on it, we see a continuous stream of life, with gradual change perpetually taking place, but with few catastrophes .... In social history we find in every period several different kinds of social and economic organisation going on simultaneously in the same country, the same shire, the same town.... Each one, gentle and simple, in his commonest goings and comings, was ruled by a complicated and ever-shifting fabric of custom and law, society and politics, events at home and abroad, some of them little known by him and less understood. Our effort is not only to get what few glimpses we can of his intimate personality, but to reconstruct the whole fabric of each passing age, and see how it affected him; to get to know more in some respects than the dweller in the past himself knew about the conditions that enveloped and controlled his life.

Having stated all the difficulties, Trevelyan went on to create a masterpiece and set us all a model of how social history may be written, with his *English Social History*.

The subject flowers into all kinds of varieties, each of them affording specimens plain or coloured, exotic or simply inviting, and all rewarding to the life of the spirit. We have space only for a few examples. There is the history of literature and the arts. A few histories of literature are masterpieces in their own right: De Sanctis's history of Italian literature, for example, or Taine's history of English literature. Courthope's standard *His-*

tory of English Poetry is alive at every point to the importance of social conditions: he rightly sees literature as the social expression it is and is well aware of the way in which even form and technique, let alone content, reflect the social circumstances, as well as the literary influences, of a period. This is true too of such admirable historians of literature as Sir Leslie Stephen and W. P. Ker; read two such remarkable books as Stephen's *English Literature and Society in the Eighteenth Century*, and Ker's *Form and Style in Poetry*.

The same is true for all the arts and sciences: there are two ways of regarding their history, and these have to be kept in focus. There is the history of the art or science as a technical discipline in itself – whether architecture or music, medicine or chemistry – and there is its history viewed as a product of a given society, reflecting its demands, needs and circumstances. You may see this approach in any good history of architecture – perhaps the most social of the arts, the art in which the social element is at its highest; look at W. H. Godfrey's *Story of English Architecture*, for instance, or the histories of many crafts, such a book as M. D. Anderson's *The Medieval Carver*. There is no end to the riches to be found here; one has only to dig a little and follow the lode. Henry Adams's classic *Mont St Michel and Chartres* will take you into the heart of the Middle Ages; so will Helen Waddell's *The Wandering Scholars*.

In no subject has this approach become more conspicuous of late than in that of science – perhaps because it had more leeway to make up. The attitude of a group of the more interesting writers on science in our time – J. B. S. Haldane, J. D. Bernal, Lancelot Hogben, Julian Huxley – is dominated by this conception of their subject, science as a social expression. It may well be that they pushed this view too far, at the expense of that which regards a science in the light of its own internal development. There is in fact no necessary conflict between them; but the over-emphasis of these writers is understandable enough in the light of the innocence of older scientists about the society their work so much affected. The history of science as such had its *doyen* in Britain in Charles Singer, whose histories of biology, anatomy, medicine, and of science in general, are not only standard works on those subjects, but afford a congenial approach to them for the non-scientist.

More attention is coming to be paid in universities to the history of science. An increasing number of books attests the growth of interest in the subject and its value as a bridge between the story of society with its needs, and man's response with the development of scientific knowledge. We may begin with G. de Santillana's *The Origins of Scientific Thought, 600 B.C. to 1500 A.D.*, and go on to A. C. Crombie's two volumes on *Medieval and Early Modern Science*. A promising new survey, *The Rise of Modern Science*, offers us the first detailed survey designed both for the general reader as well as for the student. On this the first volume, Marie Boas's *The Scientific Renaissance, 1450–1630*, sees science and humanism as twin aspects of the same impulse towards knowledge. A masterly example of what we have to learn from this subject in a particular period and area is to be seen in F. R. Johnson's *Astronomical Thought in Renaissance England*, a most original and fruitful contribution to our knowledge of the Elizabethan age.

We may take such offshoots from this prolific, umbrageous tree as the history of manners and customs, sports, education, culture. We have been given by M. and C. H. B. Quennell a delightful series of histories of 'Everyday Things in England': occupations, crafts, objects in use, household implements. James Laver gives us brochures on the history of dress and costume. Or, more bulky and substantial fare, we have the Oxford volumes surveying society at different periods: *Shakespeare's England, Johnson's England, Early Victorian England*.

These things may be taken to add up to the history of culture, a category to which English historians have not much contributed. *Kulturgeschichte* we owe more to the Germans; the reason for this was partly that their age-long failure to achieve political unity made them look to linguistic and cultural unity – *Deutschtum* – for compensatory satisfaction. We owe one of the masterpieces of *Kulturgeschichte* to a Swiss, Burckhardt's *Civilisation of the Renaissance in Italy*. A distinguished example of this kind in our own time is Huizinga's *The Waning of the Middle Ages*; a Dutch scholar, situated on the frontiers of national cultures, like Burckhardt at Basel, is in a favourable situation for observing their characteristics and what they have in common. Civilization transcends frontiers; it is a plant of hardy growth; it survives a great deal. Perhaps we may regard cultural history as having been given its prime impulse by Voltaire with his *Siècle de Louis XIV*.

We cannot consider Spengler's *Decline of the West*, which had such *réclame* after the war of 1914–18, as a true specimen of this kind of history. Apart from the fact that it has greater pretensions – altogether bogus, by the way – to exhibit a morphology of culture, it is ineradicably tendentious and inspired by the gloomy genius of German *Schadenfreude*. Because the Germans were going the way to defeat, Western civilization is to be regarded as coming to an end; such is the motivation behind that heavy façade. Nor can we regard Arnold J. Toynbee's many-volumed *A Study of History*, which was much influenced by Spengler in its inception, as a true example of cultural history. Remarkable as the book is for its extraordinary range of learning and the courage and intellectual energy of the attempt, it imposes a sociological schematism, a kind of strait-jacket, upon the diversity, the rich variability, the concreteness and unpredictability of history. Toynbee imposes *his* patterns upon the subject, seeks to be a prophet and provide answers to the contemporary problems that distract us. Hence its uncritical popular success, especially in America. But this object is neither the province nor the function of history; it is indeed contrary to its nature. The whole value of the study of history resides precisely in seeing how things were, and thus possibly discerning how and why they came about. To impose a thesis upon the facts is antithetical to the true nature of history, where we should follow the facts accurately, patiently, without prejudice. Thesis-history is false history; the true historian distrusts and eschews it. Consult Richard Pares's criticism of Toynbee in *The Historian's Business* and P. Geyl's in *Encounters in History*.

The best way to read the history of one country is as part of the civilization to which it belongs: of Britain and France, for example, as part of Europe, with all their many actions and inter-actions upon each other. There are books which will give you a valuable cross-section of history in this way, such as Tout's *England and France in the Hundred Years' War*, or C. H. Haskins's *The Normans in Europe*. Reading history across the frontiers demands more knowledge and is a sophisticated approach; it is a thing to aim at and grow up to, rather than a starting-point. The ordinary reader finds it easier to read foreign history as something foreign, external to ourselves; it is more manageable, if not more comprehensible that way. Diplomatic history is an altogether less satisfactory form intellectually; it is liable to the grave defect of being history in only one dimension, the diplomatic exchanges among the powers with regard to their relations and the issues arising between them. Its material consists largely of the notes dispatched and the memoranda upon them. Naturally this leaves out of account the real forces and factors behind the situation. And to read history from these sources is apt to lead to serious distortions, like the notorious instance of A. J. P. Taylor's *Origins of the Second World War*, where this technical consideration is one reason – the others are psychological – for a fantastic and unrecognizable picture of a profoundly serious historical theme. Similar misrepresentations and distortions occurred among American 'revisionist' historians after the first world war. These had an unfortunate effect upon public opinion and ill political consequences – a malign illustration of the importance and use of history in practical affairs.

So diplomatic history should be used sparingly and critically with students at universities, since they are not in a position to know or are able to check, and are all too easily misled by sociologists and journalist-historians with their unscrupulous appeals to the gallery.

Here, also, the biographical approach will help to round out the subject, make it more human, and actually more reliable and real. It will add the dimension of life to unilateral and often otherwise unintelligible diplomatic transactions. It is better for the student to begin with a biography of, say, Castlereagh or Canning, Palmerston or Sir Edward Grey; or such a work as Samuel F. Bemis, *John Quincy Adams and the Foundations of American Foreign Policy*. The student will then be in a better position to proceed to more general works, such as the *Cambridge History of Foreign Policy* or H. C. Allen, *Great Britain and the United States: A History of Anglo-American Relations, 1783–1952*. Or, for Benjamin Franklin's missions in England and France, read Carl van Doren's admirable biography of him.

A deeper bond between one country and another, one age and another, a vast subject in itself, is Church history. Where are we to place it in our scheme? It is difficult to say; for it impinges upon, or rather includes, every other kind of history, political, constitutional, economic, local, biographical, intellectual, cultural. It has an inexhaustible interest, and nearly all the great historians have either written about it directly or had to deal with it in the course of their work: Gibbon, Hume, Macaulay, Stubbs, Froude, Maitland, besides the historians who have made it their special field. The fact is that religion is not only closely bound up with society, but has usually been one of the strongest of all bonds holding society together, in some periods as strong as the state itself. It has the further interest of a certain duality; for regarded from the point of view of society it provides the link between the secular, temporal activities of man and that other world, a timeless order, which is the reflection of the struggle of man's spirit in this. How can the history of religion, of the churches, be any other than fascinating? It deals with the lives of the most exquisite spirits among men: in our own history such men as Bede and Thomas More, Governor Bradford and Roger Williams, Richard Hooker and George Herbert, Baxter, the Wesleys, Newman. And its range is widest of all: in some periods, like the Middle Ages, it is virtually the history of civilization, and at the other end, in the smallest unit, it is half the history of the parish; for in the mighty past, it has been conterminous with the life of man.

*

A bridge of another kind between our history and the outer world is that given us by the expansion of our people, with our institutions and characteristics, overseas. They are no less inheritors of our history than we are ourselves, and as deeply affected by it. The American revolution was the upshot of centuries of struggle for liberty and self-government within this country ; the ideas that inspired it had a long pedigree from the lawyers and political thinkers of the seventeenth century and earlier. Though with the success of the revolution the United States came into being as a separate state, no one in Britain regards their history as that of a foreign country, any more than Americans are regarded as foreigners in Britain. The individual histories of the separate English-speaking peoples is tending, under the strains and dangers of our age, to merge into the general stream of their fate together as a whole. A far-seeing example of this conception was provided after the war by Sir Winston Churchill with his four-volumed *History of the English-Speaking Peoples*. In this development American history, as the story of the most powerful of those peoples, must take an even larger place. For a sympathetic and judicious introduction you cannot do better than begin with Allan Nevins's *Brief History of the United States* ; follow this up with the best general survey, Morison and Commager's *Growth of the American Republic*. On the earlier period, still the best of all such works is C. M. Andrews's *The Colonial Period of American History*. Of sectional histories excellent examples are J. T. Adams's three volumes on New England, and the new *History of the South* now in progress in twelve volumes. For the general reader J. T. Adams's *The Epic of America* still has a message.

In the field of British Empire and Commonwealth history considerable expansion has been made in the last decades. Dr J. A. Williamson has given us new light upon the early stages of expansion overseas, upon maritime enterprise and the Tudor navigators, the early colonies and oceanic history in general ; his work is original, delightful and inspired by a fine sense of imagination. A remarkable body of work has come into being from the Oxford school. There is the work of Sir Reginald Coupland, covering many tracts of the Empire, but the bulk of his original work bearing upon Africa. His little book *Raffles* and his more recent *Livingstone's Last Journey* are the best introductions to the history of British Malaya and central Africa respectively. The general reader will find his *British Anti-Slavery Movement* and *Wilberforce* as fascinating as they are instructive. Sir Keith Hancock has given us a masterly *Survey of British Commonwealth Affairs*, the best kind of contemporary history, a difficult species. His work – since he is an Australian – reminds us that contributions of importance to this subject are beginning to flow in from Canada, Australia, South Africa and New Zealand.

Now that British rule in India is over, justice is being done to its astonishing achievements, a unique episode in world history, from both sides. Witness Philip Mason's *The Men Who Ruled India: The Founders*, and its sequel, *The Rulers*, and B. B. Misra's *The Central Administration of the British East India Company, 1773–1834*. For a sympathetic treatment of a decisive career, read Sir Penderel Moon's *Warren Hastings and British India*. For the best introduction to Canadian history, read Donald Creighton's *Dominion of the North*; for South Africa, Eric Walker's *A History of Southern Africa*; on Australia, Douglas Pike's *Australia: The Quiet Continent*; and Keith Sinclair's Penguin volume, *A History of New Zealand*.

We are led to mention world history, a category in which, with the exception of Toynbee's *Survey of History*, English historians have not much ambition to shine nowadays. We must not forget however that the most popular Universal History in the Middle Ages was by an English monk, Higden's *Polychronicon*; while Sir Walter Ralegh's *History of the World* held the stage for more than a century and will always remain a quarry for splendid English prose. In the nineteenth century Ranke wrote a *Weltgeschichte*. In our own time H. G. Wells produced a celebrated *Outline of History*, an enterprise that deserves recognition. It has the characteristic qualities and defects of that writer: largeness of imagination, immense and lively energy, extensive sympathies of mind, along with superficiality and bad judgement, an impatient ignorance in things of the spirit. He is the *Encyclopédiste* of our time *par excellence*. Still, the intention was a noble one: in his own words it was

to show that *history as one whole* is amenable to a more broad and comprehensive handling than is the history of special nations and periods, a broader handling that will bring it within the normal limitations of time and energy set to the reading of an ordinary citizen. This outline deals with ages and races and nations where the ordinary history deals with reigns and pedigrees and campaigns .... History is no exception among the sciences; as the gaps fill in, the outline simplifies; as the outlook broadens, the clustering multitude of details dissolves into general laws.

But is history a science? Does it reveal general laws in operation in human affairs? These are questions that require discussion. We can only say here that the natural impulse of the historian is towards the concrete and the particular:

> To see a World in a Grain of Sand,
> And a Heaven in a Wild Flower,
> Hold Infinity in the palm of his hand,
> And Eternity in an hour.

4 History as Science and Art

At the turn of this century there was a great deal of discussion whether history was a science or an art. The discussion had been going on for some time on the Continent, particularly in Germany where it became part of a famous controversy among philosophers and historians, the *Methodenstreit*. In England it was brought to a head by Bury's celebrated challenge in his inaugural lecture at Cambridge: 'History is a science, no less and no more.' He followed it up with the declaration that 'so long as history was regarded as an art, the sanctions of truth and accuracy could not be severe', and, even more rigorously, 'I may remind you that history is not a branch of literature.' York Powell at Oxford thought much the same thing:

Modern history today, then, shall mean what might perhaps be called the New History, as distinct from the Old History. The New History is history written by those who believe that history is not a department of *belles-lettres* and just an elegant, instructive and amusing narrative, but a branch of science. This science, like many other sciences, is largely the creation of the nineteenth century. It deals with the condition of masses of mankind living in a social state. It seeks to discover the laws that govern these conditions and bring about the changes we call Progress and Decay, and Development and Degeneracy – to understand the processes that gradually or suddenly make up and break up those political and economic agglomerations we call States – to find out the circumstances affecting the various tendencies that show their power at various times. Style and the needs of a popular audience have no more to do with history than with law or astronomy.

That point of view became the dominant one in the universities in this century and it has had important effects, both good and bad.

To take some of the good first. The insistence that history is
a science, with rigorous standards and methods, led to greater
care in ascertaining and stating the truth, to a watchful emphasis upon accuracy at every point, in examining evidence
and arriving at conclusions from it, a constant awareness of the
dangers of bias and attempts on every side to counteract it. All
this made history more difficult to write – at any rate, well –
and less interesting to read. On the other hand, since this point
of view attached little importance to literary quality it meant
a large increase in the amount of history books turned out by
people who did not know how to write. Never was there such
a quantity of raw hunks of historical research, malformed, un-
digested, indigestible, as poured forth from the presses. One
recalls Swift's contempt, much less deserved, for the antiquarian
works of Madox, for whom he had been passed over for the
post of Historiographer Royal.

There was a further advantage from the point of view of
historical teaching and examination at the universities. 'Unscientific', 'literary' history – the ideal reading for the leisured
country gentleman – was apt to become a 'soft option'. Ambling
through Gibbon or Hume, Macaulay or Carlyle, deep in an arm-
chair with the feet on the mantelpiece, was no way of training
the mind. Something more gritty and rigorous was necessary;
something that might take the place of the grammatical and
linguistic discipline of the Classics, now that history was coming to displace the Classics as the most popular Arts subject in
education. As early as 1853, Froude, then at the beginning of
his career and in time to become a distinguished 'literary' historian, especially obnoxious to the scientific school, stressed
just this point in an interesting manifesto in *Oxford Essays*. His
contribution was a proposal for a History School, which should
get down to the study of the Statutes of the Realm and of the
documents and texts from which history is written. Under
Stubbs, one of the ablest editors of texts, this came about at
Oxford, and other universities followed suit. The growth of the
history schools has been one of the marked features in university education since : thousands of students have passed through
them. No doubt the training they got in accuracy, in assessing

evidence and making up their minds upon it, in common-sense judgement about public affairs, must count for something in the life of the community.

But – in historical writing? Trevelyan thinks that 'Macaulay and Carlyle themselves would have been even better historians than they were if they had been through an academic course of history such as they could have got if they had lived at the end of the nineteenth century instead of at the beginning.' I wonder. They might have been less biased, more accurate; they would certainly have been less passionate, less coloured, less vivid. Perhaps nothing would have reduced such personalities as theirs to the carefully neutral grey tints of Gardiner, the dry, repressed anatomics of Firth. And yet Firth, as a person, was a most vigorous and humorous human being. The reaction certainly went too far.

Its most deleterious consequence was that it made a disjunction between academic history, which exemplified good standards of scholarship but was not read by the public, and the kind of history that the public fell for. If people with good university standards would not, or could not, write in such a way as to be readable, the general public fell into the hands of charlatans, the Chestertons and Bellocs – or rather it was the Chestertons and Bellocs that fell into the hands of the public. Nothing could be worse; the public got a completely distorted view of the country's past, or a reading of it that simply made nonsense; James II treated as a hero, the revolution of 1688 as a mistake, Elizabeth as a pathological puppet in the hands of a Cecil, the Reformation – which in fact made our fortune as a people – regarded as a disaster. It may be said by a sceptic that the dominant tradition of our history is so strong that we can well afford for opposition views to be put forward. But – even if they are thoroughly silly? Whatever nonsense they make? I should say that the proper aim of historical study is to get as near the truth as we can, putting what is to be said for the Reformation, or the French revolution or the Russian, or the British Empire, as well as what is to be said against. And as one who for some years read the scholarship papers of candidates for entry to the university, I know the kind of harm that can be done by reading history from that kind of book. (I am not saying anything against Belloc and Chesterton as poets, essayists, novelists; I admire their work in those forms; they were men of genius – but they were not historians.)

In our time a salutary reaction has come about against the too rigorously academic and 'scientific' view of history; it no longer has the field to itself even at the universities, and once more the best academic writers are writing for a wider public. The historian who more than any other has won this battle is Trevelyan, who all his life has stood for this view. He has told us how the 'reaction against "literary history", as it was scornfully called, was rampant fifty years ago, when I commenced historian'. Following him, a whole school of writers has come into existence, John Buchan with his historical biographies, Arthur Bryant, professional historians such as Sir John Neale and his *Queen Elizabeth*, J. A. Williamson, C. V. Wedgwood and Dr J. H. Plumb – all of them with a university background and academic standards, who yet are read with enjoyment by a wide public. In the United States we have such shining examples as Samuel Eliot Morison, a truly great historian, Allan Nevins and Garrett Mattingly, to point the way.

It is easy to see now what the main influences were that made academic historians insist upon the scientific character of their subject. There was the increasing insistence of a scientific age upon exactness, accuracy, objectivity; there was – somewhat paradoxically, in the light of these standards – the influence of German thinkers; most important of all, there was the prestige of the physical sciences with their achievements in theory and practice to their credit. As Trevelyan says:

Science had transmuted the economic and social life of mankind, and had revolutionised the religious and cosmological outlook of the educated world. These astonishing achievements of physical science led many historians, fifty years ago, to suppose that the value and importance of history would be greatly enhanced if history was called a science, and if it adopted scientific methods and ideals and none others.

He then goes on to declare his own point of view:

I believe that this analogy was faulty. For the study of mankind does not resemble the study of the physical properties of atoms, or the life history of animals. If you find out about one atom, you have found out about all atoms, and what is true of the habits of one robin is roughly true of the habits of all robins. But the life history of one man, or even of many individual men, will not tell you the life history of other men. Moreover you cannot make a full scientific analysis of the life history of any one man. Men are too complicated, too spiritual, too various, for scientific analysis; and the life history of millions cannot be inferred from the history of single men. History, in fact, is more a matter of rough guessing from all the available facts. And it deals with intellectual and spiritual forces which cannot be subjected to any analysis that can properly be called scientific.

Now we have the two opposing points of view. 'History is a science, no less and no more' (Bury). 'History is not a systematic branch of knowledge' (Eduard Meyer). What are we to think as between them? What is the truth of the matter?

It is proper to point out here that the word 'science' in modern usage has become increasingly restricted to the exact sciences, those which on the basis of demonstrable truths or observed facts, systematically classified, are susceptible of general laws, from which reliable conclusions may be drawn from like premises. Of these disciplines the oustanding examples are the physical sciences. Originally the word 'science' meant knowledge or learning, or any branch of it; as in the usage, 'moral sciences', or 'theological science' – though the conclusions to be drawn from the latter, whatever the premises, could hardly be regarded as reliable, or in any way exact. May it be that even the exact sciences are themselves not always so exact? The discovery of new phenomena is constantly bringing about the recasting of the theory. And what of the social sciences, such disciplines as economics, anthropology, psychology? I can only say here that it is not desirable to restrict the use of the word 'science' to too narrow a sense. The social sciences have not the cast-iron regularity of the physics of the nineteenth century – nor for that matter has physics in the twentieth century. What *is* it that historians have in mind when they claim, or disclaim, history as a science? I think they have at the back of their minds an idea of exactness, dependable objectivity (though in an ultimate sense what objectivity is there even in physics?), a certain capacity for being systematized as knowledge.

Most of us would agree that historical research and study profit from their methods being as scientific as possible, i.e. exact, rigorous, systematic. In modern historical study there has grown up a much more accurate testing of sources, altogether fuller correlation of evidence. What were but tools of the historian's trade have become subjects in themselves, like palaeography or diplomacy, the study of handwritings, the forms of documents. Archaeology has become a world of learning in itself, with its own scientific methods, and with inexhaustible new fields of information to add to history. Air photography aids in the campaign that the historian wages with the past, recovering every scrap that he can, observing the traces of previous cultivation under the soil, lost villages and towns, encampments and mounds, the relics of earlier civilizations. There are the further aids that we derive from statistics, from economics and notably from geography.

Even so, even in the realm of historical method, there is a non-scientific element that is just as important. There is the feeling for the material such as any good craftsman must have for the medium he is working in, the potter for the clay, the mason for the stone, the needle-woman for the texture of her stuff. There is sympathy of mind, love of the subject in and for itself, that kind of understanding that tells one what to beware of and what to look for; one derives all sorts of unconscious aids from the practice of one's craft, as with poetry or gardening. There is in the end, intuition; that leap of the mind that suddenly suggests the explanation. One cannot analyse it psychologically here, even if it is possible to analyse it satisfactorily at all; but it is liable to come, one cannot foretell the moment, when the mind is in a certain condition of preparedness, sometimes when one has worked oneself to a standstill along purely intellectual lines. Perhaps it is analogous to Keats's 'negative capability': that condition of receptiveness when the subtler and more spontaneous apparatus of the unconscious comes into play and takes charge, in a fortunate moment crystallizing what had been confused and uncertain before. Is it any different essentially from the way a scientific theory comes to birth? These things are complicated, and when one gets into them the difference between one thing and another narrows down. If they turn out to be curiously alike at bottom, there is, as against the difficulty we have in drawing our distinctions clearly, the consoling thought of the unity of human knowledge.

Again, with regard to the *content* of history, the matter in itself, the situation is complex. I do not accept the exclusiveness of either Bury on one side or Trevelyan on the other. There *is* a scientific element in history; the point here is to isolate it, to say what it is and what it is not. History in any case is not an assemblage of individual facts without connection, a rag-bag of things that have happened anyhow. All historians, of whatever school, have drawn conclusions and made generalizations from what they were describing. That fact gives us a clue to what must be the nature of the subject: it is descriptive like other social sciences, anthropology for instance, but there are generalizations from the facts viewed in sequence. The facts of history are not isolated, concrete, like pebbles on a beach; they are connected by skeins of consequence in every direction. One state of affairs leads to another, arises out of an earlier one; they are connected causally. The fact that the cause is often not simple or unilateral does not mean that it is not there; it only means that it is more difficult to disentangle and estimate. That again is one of the advantages of the social sciences: they are not rigid and schematic; they have the subtlety, the suppleness and flexibility of life itself. All that they have to offer must be viewed in terms of life; that is the ultimate reality and their final claim. Life is the *ultima ratio* of history, not something outside it, some abstraction of the mind that yet makes transcendent claims, something invented.

Yet this does not mean that there are not systematic elements in history – because it does not form one system in itself, any more than life does. There are such elements, capable of scientific analysis; the population of a country, its number and character, is a matter of obvious importance in its history and to any historian writing it. How shall he proceed in the matter?

My answer is by two methods, which dovetail in with one another; one is intellectual and scientific, the other is intuitive and aesthetic. They do not conflict; they complement each other, they illuminate each other. There is the whole secret of history, of historical writing and study; it lies in its duality of vision, an intimate and constant two-mindedness, or, if you like, duplicity of mind. It does not study the world through a microscope or a telescope; it has two eyes always upon the subject, one analytical and scientific, the other selective and aesthetic. Gibbon has his statistics and his generalizations, but he also gives one the picture of life and the feel of the thing.

Whether the one element or the other predominates depends on the subject and what one wants of it. The systematic and scientific element is at its largest in early human and prehistory. It is of greater importance in dealing with mass phenomena than with the individual. Though even with the individual there is a scientific element – why otherwise psychology?; and in dealing with masses, conversely, there is a value-element – how otherwise patriotism, loyalty, self-sacrifice? These things are not easy to disentangle, but that is no reason why we should give up hope of ordering them, relapse into an easy scepticism where there are no distinctions and no understanding the layout of things; or, on the other hand, rush hopelessly to embrace one or the other of two exclusive choices. We have to carry both in our mind all the time if we are to understand history. Then the rewards of ambivalence are immeasurable.

Back to population, the example we took. If we are to understand that factor in the history we are dealing with we need some statistics and some ethnology – a little of each will probably go a long way with the historian. In any case it will be better than mere impressions – though impressions too have their place. The impressions of Herodotus, as anthropologists now realize, have a good deal of historical value. Sir John Myres tells us that

History, in its common and more popular sense, is the study of Man's dealings with other men, and the adjustment of working relations between human groups. But there is a larger sense, in which Human History merges in Natural History, and studies the dealings of Man with Nature.... Man's prehistory merges in the pageant of the animal world, and of the planet-wide arena on which it has been in progress. Mountain and sea-basin too have their history. Their geographical distribution has varied in immemorial years.... To see how the stage itself was set for this pageant, we must look back beyond the moment when the first characters enter it. For it has been Nature, rather than Man, hitherto, in almost every scene, that has determined where the action shall lie.

It is obvious that here the scientific element is at its highest; indeed there is no understanding of all that tract of history except through science; they are practically co-terminous. In these early stages human history is determined by geology and geography. We reach back to 'more strongly marked contrasts in the composition and structure of its rocks, which have so profoundly affected the habitability and the human prosperity of each component region, through the peculiar distribution of its plants and animals, and eventually of its breeds of Man'.

History is not then solely 'a matter of rough guessing'. There are areas where we can do nothing but guess, for lack of evidence; there are other areas where guessing, or imaginative interpretation, is the appropriate technique. Over and beyond these there are places where the right thing to do is to collect figures, establish generalizations, observe tendencies which have something of the regularity of law. Nothing is more remarkable to a discerning student of British history than the dualism of English and Celtic characteristics in the people: the extremism, the vivacity and temperament of the one, the reliability, the dogged qualities, the imagination, the sense of moderation of the other. There is no doubt, fortunately, which is the dominant. Anyone with discernment can observe these strains coming out in our people and in their history; and we can say that without involving ourselves in the crudities of racialism. The stock counts for something, and a scientific ethnology is the way to assess it.

Without going out of our depth we can see that in quite ordinary tracts of history some generalization is possible. Take the effects of inflation or deflation upon the economic circumstances of a society, the social relations of classes. We can ob-

serve with some regularity in history what the effects of an
inflation are and predict with some probability what they will
be. An inflation disturbs and throws out of gear the accustomed
dues from one class to another ; that which depends upon fixed
monetary payments loses and goes down economically ; those
groups whose assets are in real property, mainly land – particularly if their ownership is absolute and their capital at their
own disposition and therefore flexible – gain hand over fist at
such a time. We may see the consequences at work in England
during the Reformation period, or in France during the revolution. The consequences of deflation are still more regular and
observable : gain for the rentiers and for the holders of fixed
securities and payments, restriction of production, unemploy-
ment. Debasing the currency is a well-trodden path historically,
and its consequences are fairly predictable. There seems no
reason why we should not regard Gresham's law as an historical law as much as an economic one.

There are other general tendencies observable in history, not
only in economic history – though there they may be, as Bury
thought, at their most regular – tendencies that approximate to
laws. When peoples arrive at a certain degree of cohesion,
strength and self-consciousness, it seems to be impossible for
other peoples to hold them down permanently. That nationalism is an irresistible force is a conclusion to be drawn from
history. I do not wish to say that history has any one *terminus
ad quem* ; that would be to suffer from the finality-mindedness
of people like Hegel, who thought the final stage in the realiza-
tion of the self in the world was the Prussian State. That kind
of mentality is really a lag-over from the theological way of
thinking of an earlier age – theology with God left out. Yet even
Hegel thought that there was a progressive self-realization at
work in history ; and in spite of all sorts of disillusionments and
set-backs there does seem to be an irresistible impulse towards
self-government in human society.

It went against the sense of history for Britain to go on with
the attempt to govern Ireland in the nineteenth century, as it
was a mistake to hold on to the American Colonies in
the eighteenth century. The latter were already ripe, in-

deed overripe, for self-government, though few at the time perceived it. This became evident with the extraordinary speed and competence with which the new United States put forth all the organs and integuments of a great power ; never has she had such a galaxy of political genius and talent. In any case the American Colonies would have had to assume vital independence a decade later, when Britain was involved in a struggle for her existence against the French revolution and Napoleon. The pity of it was that the British governing class did not read the signs of the times and recognize the ineluctable trend towards independence and self-government. In this century they have done better in regard to India and accepted the movement of the Indian people towards self-government with good will. The people may be less well governed, but they may be happier governing themselves less well. The impulse is irresistible ; the only point at issue is how and in what circumstances we can best hand over.

History seems to indicate that the right moment is when a people has arrived at a sufficient degree of political maturity to take their affairs into their own hands. The same general law brought the attempts of Napoleon and of Hitler to rule the whole of Europe to nothing, and we hope will do the same for anybody else who tries the same thing. The general conclusion to be drawn from European history is that no one power is strong enough to rule all the rest. Therefore the sensible thing (i.e. what the sense of history indicates) is some federal system that may enable us to work together in cooperation. On the basis of a knowledge of history we can look into the nearer future and see something of the shape of things that is emerging. And that knowledge is the best aid to knowing what we can usefully achieve in our turn.

We are here verging upon the fundamental question of determinism and free will that crops up in some guise in every age and mental climate, though it usually has a theological colouring in periods given to theological speculation. We may hope to deal with it as it affects history in the next chapter. It is sufficient for the moment to point out that man's success – indeed his universal triumph, compared with other animals – is due to his learning how to conform to the necessities of nature. In nature's service is his freedom – if it is hardly perfect freedom. (Perhaps perfect freedom is only to be found in service to an idea, an idea of the non-existent.) As Sir John Myres says :

It is man's inertia, rather than any initiative, his obstinate reluctance to abandon a mode of life once adopted, his recourse to any compromise – 'rather to endure the ills we have than fly to others that we know not of' – and, in the result, his unique ability to conquer Nature by reasoned conformity with Nature's ways, that differentiates him from all animals but those, such as horse and dog, in which he has apprehended and elicited faculties remotely analogous to his own.

(I am sorry that Sir John should have omitted that sage animal, the cat.)

The distinction between the mass and the individual has an importance for the discussion of how far there is a scientific element in history, analytical and intellectual, as opposed to the descriptiveness and intuitions of art. It is to mass-phenomena that scientific analysis is most applicable. The individual is largely unpredictable ; but even he is not wholly unpredictable. Otherwise there would be no point in psychology ; or where would be the point in 'the knowledge of human nature', universally admitted to be useful? If we know something of his desires, predilections, characteristics – still more if we know something about his complexes, for they reveal the operations of the sub-conscious – we know a good deal of how he is likely to behave. With the mass our knowledge is a good deal more certain ; for with a large number of people the individual differences and idiosyncrasies even out and they will behave very largely in accordance with the forces that impinge upon them. Threaten the survival of a nation and they will fight as one man. History is full of such instances : the Dutch fighting against Philip II's tyranny, against Louis XIV's threat to overwhelm them, the French against reactionary Europe in 1792. Humiliate a people and you can expect a fairly certain reaction. Put down the wages of a class of workers, or attempt to take away the property of a given social group – and the reactions will be fairly reliable, though their character and effectiveness will depend upon conditions, the strength of the group, the resistance it meets with and so on.

What one is chiefly dealing with in the realm of mass-action in history – and that is to the fore in political, economic, social, constitutional history, in the relations of states – is the public aspect of people's behaviour. One is not concerned primarily with their behaviour as fathers or children, as sportsmen or clubbable men, as artists or cultivators of their gardens. All that belongs to the private sphere of their conduct, and hardly concerns history at all – except perhaps social history and, even then, only for what it adds up to. It is precisely in this sphere of the public behaviour of the mass that one can generalize best, and even forecast to some extent. If geology and history provide the background to human history we may change the metaphor to liken mass-action to the warp and woof of the texture, individual action to individual threads woven into it. They may have different colours and even pursue an erratic course across the patterns, but they remain part of the texture. To vary the image : individuals cannot think themselves off the map, or rather they may think themselves off it (many with philosophical and other-worldly interests have done), but they remain all the same upon it. They are conditioned, even determined, by their physical and social environment. Man is a social construct ; he is what race and country, region and family, church and school and economic grouping make him. As such, he is susceptible of analysis and even a fair amount of prediction as to his general course, though its particular lines may be fluid and flexible within the pattern.

This, then, is the perspective proper to history in which to view the actions of the individual. There is danger in theorizing too much about history ; any particular 'theory of history' is liable to be too schematic ; the point comes when the rich and undisciplined variety of human events is forced into the restrictive framework of the (very fallible) theorist. And that is to go against the very nature of history. On the other hand, we must not fall into the too comfortable ways of historical scepticism and say that there is no knowing how human beings will act or react, that there is no rhyme or reason in it, that there are no regular tendencies or rules and no generalization is possible.

There is some system in history and it is at its highest when one observes the movements of masses. Even the most sceptical of philosophers, Hume, thought: 'What depends upon few persons is, in a great measure, to be ascribed to chance, or secret and unknown causes; what arises from a great number may often be accounted for by determinate and known causes.' The 'laws' of history, then, are of the nature of statistical generalizations: in dealing with one individual little calculation is possible; in dealing with a large number, one may even draw graphs, as in economics – provided one takes one's graphs with a pinch of common sense.

Dilthey, the modern philosopher most congenial to the historian, with the possible exception of Hume, drew a marked contrast between *Naturwissenschaft* and *Geisteswissenschaft*, between the natural sciences and the humane studies. He thought that the empiricists and positivists of the nineteenth century, Mill and Spencer and Comte, were wrong in assuming that the methods and presuppositions of the natural sciences could be transferred substantially unchanged to the human studies. Dilthey thought, Professor Hodges tells us, that 'the human studies are knowledge in a sense in which natural science is not, because physical objects as known to us are merely appearances, while minds are "real realities" known to us as they are in themselves.' This is not an attempt to deny either the reality of the external world or the real triumphs of natural science in investigating it. There are obvious ways in which we know physical nature better than we know man or society. We can describe and analyse, explain and predict, with far greater precision in the former than in the latter, nor does our knowledge of nature depend in any degree upon human testimony borne by unscientific witnesses. On the other hand, we cannot enter into the being of physical things and processes as we can with human beings and societies, where sympathetic insight, based on the identity of nature between ourselves and what we study, enables us to appreciate not only the external movements and changes, but the motives producing them and their meaning for the people concerned. It is this that makes Dilthey call the human studies a knowledge of reality in a sense in which natural science is not.

The data of history not only are manifestations of mind, but are perceived as such, and this makes an epistemological difference between historical study and natural science. The scientist observes things and processes, but perceives no activity in them, no dynamic relationships. What he learns of their causal connections is learned by hypothesis and experiment and remains in the form of abstract law. But the manifestations of mind are instinct with the life from which they sprang and upon which they continually react. We cannot observe them at all without seeing them as parts of a dynamic process, and this is the very thing that is meant by calling them 'historical'. 'Mind understands only what it has created. Nature, the object of natural science, embraces that reality which is produced independently of the activity of the mind. Everything upon which man by acting has set his stamp forms the object of the human studies.'

I think that Dilthey makes too rigid a contrast between the methods of the natural sciences and of the humane studies. For we must remember that in the simplest and most fundamental way historical method and scientific method are one and the same. In both you proceed from the assembling of particular facts to generalizations, and from generalizations back to the facts. In both science and history you do not start from nothing; you begin with common sense and with a working hypothesis; as you go on you modify your hypothesis in accordance with the evidence. And so generalization is built up and theories which illuminate the facts, in the light of which they may be interpreted and often gain significance. But always, in both science and history, the generalization is subject to revision in the light of new evidence; it is constantly being moulded and remoulded in keeping with the facts.

It is this that provides the defence for the detailed research that many people question in the case of history. What is the use of all the elaborate research into the wardrobe of Edward II, they ask; or into the distinctions between one kind of seal and another, great seal, privy seal, ordinary seal or signet; or between one kind of writ and another? It is important to keep a sense of proportion, and there are historians who do not have much of it, just as there must be scientists with none or very little. But it does not seem to occur to the man in the street to question the use of the same kind of elaborate and detailed research, that may not be leading anywhere in particular, in the case of science. Whereas the whole point – and the defence for it – is the same in the case of both history and science: it is essential for the subject as a whole to establish absolute accuracy and complete information, or as near as one can get to it, in regard to detail and in all parts of the subject. That is a process which must always go on and be pursued, otherwise the generalizations are faulty, the subject as a whole must inevitably suffer.

To my mind this is a complete answer to those who question the use of historical research, or for that matter of scientific research. The case is the same in regard to both. We know that some researchers view things disproportionately; to some extent that is in the nature of things; workers engaged in intensive study of a narrow field are apt to think it more important than it probably is. But one never can tell what may turn up, and, anyhow, they might not otherwise go on. The remedy is clear: it is best to have a good general view of one's subject as well as to do a piece of detailed research into it. One needs to keep the two in focus, and each will have a salutary influence on the other: the detailed research for being viewed in a wider perspective, the general approach for having the caution, the accuracy and exactness of statement generated by the experience of research. I am all in favour of the good academic historian being able to write for the general reader on one side as well as for his own professional public on the other.

To return: there are on the other hand some branches of science where the methods of study are largely historical. For example, geology; the establishment of successive geological periods follows much the same method as that of historical documentation, only the documents are rocks and stones. Or in the case of palaeontology, the study of primitive organisms: of which the purpose is to establish the succession of series, by methods which must be historical. And so we move into the sphere of prehistory and then history proper.

We have seen in this chapter that there is a *Naturwissenschaft* element in the study of history; that is to say, that there are areas of the subject where a scientific approach is appropriate, in studying the physical and geographical environment and their impact upon the human story, in analysing economic and social forces and their influence upon the configurations and behaviour of masses of men in society; in understanding many aspects of mass-action and even in the psychological interpretation of the individual.

In the long run all these intellectual aids are but external; the inner spirit of history, the genius of the thing, is elsewhere – it is in the spirit of man, the flame of life itself. The appropriate rendering of that can only be given by art. Even Dilthey allows a large part to the purely intellectual and analytical element in the historian's labour, 'testing the meaning and value of sources, filling gaps, resolving inconsistencies, detecting causal connections, and so working out a coherent and well-grounded narrative. But he is only doing on a large scale what we all do when we understand the sayings and doings of our neighbours.' That is to say, the historian's business is, like the novelist's, to render life in its proper terms, by common-sense interpretation, knowledge of human nature from experience and understanding, by sympathetic insight, imagination. Still, 'where imaginative understanding can be turned into or supplemented by causal explanation, this ought to be done, and if there is sense in speaking of the progress of history towards the rank of a science, it must mean in great part this very progress from imaginative to intellective apprehension, from the vision of what is natural to the recognition of what is regular. In so far as this process goes on, the gap between history and sociology will be narrowed, and the dream of the positivists, that history could ultimately be made into applied sociology, represents the goal of such an advance, a goal none the less genuine because it will never be fully attained.'

In the end, as Dilthey thought, it is the imaginative process of understanding that gives life and meaning to the rest. For that is the way to apprehend life – and history records for us life as it has been lived by man. Its essence therefore is in the concrete fact, the manifold variety of events and happenings that once took place in the real world. The historian's business is to narrate them, to re-create them. To do that he needs to be an artist. The process of historical recreation is not essentially different from that of the poet or novelist, except that his imagination must be subordinated sleeplessly to the truth. He must consent to be ruled by the evidence and never go against it. It is an austere and searching vocation.

It is not for nothing that the way of intuitive understanding, of imaginative insight, has always in the end been that of the great historians. Herodotus and Thucydides, Tacitus and Livy, Clarendon, Hume and Gibbon, Macaulay and Carlyle were all artists and among the foremost writers of their time. And however much they may be supplemented by scientific methods and acquisitions – the contribution these have to make will certainly grow – there will always remain history as an art.

5 Historical Thinking

The nineteenth century saw a profound intellectual revolution, the full effects of which are only being worked out in our time. It was intimately connected with history; it was indeed mainly concerned with history; we may say that it was historical in character. It brought about a new way of looking at things that was evolutionary by nature; that is, it regarded them as *developing*, in ceaseless process of change. The actual process of change was not fully understood; Darwin's particular theory of evolution by natural selection was one hypothesis as to how change came about in the realm of natural science. But the chief advance was to think of things in terms of change at all, and not merely that, but to think of change as having causes. Trying to analyse what those causes are has been a prime object of intellectual effort in both natural and social sciences ever since.

It is impossible to exaggerate the difference this approach has made in every sphere. You can see it most simply if you take an eighteenth-century work on history and compare it with the modern approach. If you take, for example, Lord Bolingbroke's *Letters on History* – very typical of the mind of his age – you will see that he thinks of successive periods as a series of water-tight compartments, with nothing to account for the transition from one to another except catastrophes or breakdowns. No conception of development or progressive change at all. (I use the word 'progressive' to mean producing something different or new, not in the nineteenth-century sense implying anything necessarily better, or moving towards some given end or other.) Now we think of things as in a ceaseless flux; and though that makes them more difficult to grasp, we

are at any rate nearer to understanding them, or at least describing them as they are.

The effects of evolutionary theory have gone much further
than this. They have been such as completely to recast our view
of the universe, of man and his place in it, of the descent of
man – the controversy about this last was merely the most
spectacular phase of the discussion, the one that had most pub-
licity at the time, so to say, and not necessarily the most important. It has had the effect of undermining the absolute claims
of religion and metaphysics, of ethics and law. It seems that in
an uncertain world only the absoluteness of aesthetics remains,
and possibly that of mathematical and logical propositions.
The idea of God has been rendered superfluous ; those who wish
to retain something of the old framework of thought have been
reduced either to a very shadowy and tenuous concept removed
to an abstract world having little to do with human affairs, or
else to a virtual identification with the human, indistinguishable
from practical humanism. (Mere superstitions, of course, remain.) The evolutionary view of the universe has brought us to
an almost completely relativist way of looking at things. Is
there any absolute truth to be found anywhere, and if so,
where?

There is no use running away from the facts or trying to re-
furbish the old dogmas, half explaining them away, half polish-
ing them up to look like new. There is no help for us that way.

We can only face our difficulties and try to think our way
through them. There are too many writers whose chief anxiety
seems to be not to give themselves away. The result is that they
are no help to us. They merely repeat what is safe to say because it has been said before. But we do not know what they
think, if anything. I can only give you what I really think about
these difficult problems, however inadequate and provisional it
may be. There is this to encourage one : that nobody at any
rate has entirely satisfied my mind on these questions, or said
the final word about them, and therefore I must try to think
out the answers myself.

Back to evolution and its relation to history! Some people
seem to think that the study of history, the whole concept of

history, was revolutionized under the influence of the ideas worked out, notably by Darwin, in the field of natural science.
R. G. Collingwood thinks on the other hand that evolutionary
ideas in science were developed under the impact of history.

History had by now established itself as a science, that is, a
progressive inquiry in which conclusions are solidly and demon-
stratively established. It had thus been proved by experiment that
scientific knowledge was possible concerning objects that were
constantly changing. Once more, the self-consciousness of man, in
this case the corporate self-consciousness of man, his historical
consciousness of his own corporate doings, provided a clue to his
thoughts about nature. The historical conception of scientifically
knowable change or process was applied, under the name of evolution, to the natural world.

There is more in this emphasis of Collingwood's than is generally realized, though I do not go all the way with him. Marxists are in the habit of pointing proudly to the fact that Marx
with his ideas of social evolution was at least co-eval with Darwin, and thought of himself as a kind of Darwin of the social
sciences. *The Origin of Species* appeared in 1859, *Das Kapital*
in 1867. But Newman's *Essay on the Development of Christian
Doctrine*, with its interesting, if arbitrarily restricted, theory of
the evolution of dogma, was published in 1845. But before him
was Coleridge, and before him Herder. I mention these things
only in order to make clear that there is little point in trying
to track down who was first with the expression of a new idea ;
every historian knows that new ideas crop up in various places
at about the same time, as if in response to new demands upon
men.

In fact, evolutionary theory in science and what has been
called, modestly and sensibly in England, 'the historical method' (*Historismus*, or historicism, in Germany) are twin developments of the same fundamental movement in thought,
which characterized the 'mental climate' of the nineteenth century. Bury saw that clearly :

The growth of historical study in the nineteenth century has been
determined and characterised by the same general principle which
has underlain the simultaneous developments of the study of nature,

namely the *genetic* idea. The 'historical' conception of nature, which has produced the history of the solar system, the story of the earth, the genealogies of telluric organisms, and has revolutionised natural science, belongs to the same order of thought as the conception of human history as a continuous, genetic, causal process – a conception which has revolutionised historical research and made it scientific.

He goes on to explain that 'for history it meant that the present condition of the human race is simply and strictly the result of a causal series (or set of causal series) – a continuous succession of changes, where each state arises causally out of the preceding; and that the business of historians is to trace this genetic process, to explain each change, and ultimately to grasp the complete development of humanity'. He points out that 'the predominant importance of the masses was the assumption which made it possible to apply evolutionary principles to history ... for it is only when the masses are moved into the foreground that regularity, uniformity and law can be conceived as applicable'. It will be remembered that this is the very point that I laboured in the previous chapter; it is pleasant to know that Bury had the same thought.

The most notable attempt to work out evolutionary ideas in the realm of social science was that of Marxism. And certainly it has been the most influential in the effect it has had in many fields, in politics and economics, in history, sociology, literary criticism, and even, with some writers, in natural science itself, where its application much bothered the mind of Lenin. He wrote an unreadable book on the subject: *Materialism and Empirio-Criticism*, a work of dogmatism and intellectual tactics rather than a contribution to knowledge – also characteristic of the Russian habit of imposing an orthodoxy on other people's minds.

To confine ourselves to the Marxist view of history. Neither Marx nor Engels ever gave a complete exposition of what they thought on this subject; they never even devoted an essay to it. And yet it underlies their whole point of view about politics and society. What we have are various passages in different works of Marx, with some glosses on them afterwards by Engels. These

are enough to make clear their point of view, and in any case
the works themselves are illustrations and developments of it.

The first point to grasp is that the Marxist view came into
being as a direct reaction against Hegel's 'Idealism'. Hegel
thought of the universe in an evolutionary way, but as the self-
development and the self-realization of the primal 'Idea'. His
was an idealist philosopher's way of looking at things, and there
never was a more transcendental philosophy more absolute in
character or more totalitarian in its claims. Quite early on, in
the rude manner of a clever pupil turning on his master, Marx
asked:

Do these gentlemen think that they can understand the first word
of history as long as they exclude the relations of man to nature,
natural science and industry? Do they believe that they can com-
prehend any epoch without grasping the industry of the period, the
immediate methods of production in actual life? ... Just as they
separate the soul from the body, and themselves from the world,
so they separate history from natural science and industry, so they
find the birth-place of history not in the gross material production
on earth, but in the misty cloud formation of heaven.

This was a salutary reversal of emphasis, and it shows how
Marx's view came to be described as 'the materialist conception of history', or 'historical materialism'. Actually Marx dis-
agreed with the mechanical materialism of Feuerbach, with his
dictum *Der Mensch ist was er isst* (Man is what he eats) and
criticized Feuerbach's materialist view of religion on the proper
ground that he had failed to perceive that man is the product
of his social relations and that religion itself is a social out-
growth. Marx suggests, rather than creates, a more comprehensive development of his view with the following:

In changing the modes of production, mankind changes all its
social relations. The hand mill creates a society with the feudal
lord; the steam mill a society with the industrial capitalist. The
same men who establish social relations in conformity with their
material production also create principles, ideas and categories in
conformity with their social relations.... All such ideas and categories are therefore historical and transitory products.

That opens up some searching questions, which we must return to later. Are the ideas and standards brought into existence by a given set of historical circumstances at a certain time confined to those conditions and that time for their validity? Are we reduced to a complete historical scepticism? The actual influence of Marxism in practical affairs has been in part towards a sort of nihilism on one side, the product of scepticism with regard to absolute standards, and fanaticism on the other. The two are not unconnected, as can be seen by reference to Nazism. Marx himself never said anything on this ultimate issue ; though his own behaviour was the reverse of that of a man who did not believe in absolute standards, while it is equally clear that he was not intellectually a sceptic. Still his silence is disquieting ; any discerning student of Marx is impelled to the view that he was disquieted himself and that was why he kept silence about it.

For the present let us finish our sketch of his view in his own words:

With the change in the social relations by means of which individuals produce, that is, in the social relations of production, and with the alteration and development of the material means of production, the powers of production are also transformed. The relations of production collectively form those social relations which we call society, and a society with definite degrees of historical development.... Ancient society, feudal society, bourgeois society, are simply instances of this collective result of the complexes of relations of production, each of which marks an important step in the historical development of mankind.

This is the way Germans write and think – Hegel is far worse ; one can at least see what it is that Marx is saying. To go a stage further with him :

On the various forms of property, on the conditions of social existence, there rises an entire superstructure of various and peculiarly formed sensations, illusions, methods of thought and views of life. The whole class fashions and moulds them from out of their material foundations and their corresponding social relations. The single individual, in whom they converge through tradition and education, is apt to imagine that they constitute the real determining causes and the point of departure of his action.

With this last point we may readily agree. Ordinary human beings never think of themselves as social products, of what they are and do and think – in that order – as being largely conditioned by the circumstances brought to bear upon them, the forces and factors, environmental and inherited, that have made them what they are. The more unconscious they are of this, the more conditioned their behaviour and what passes for their thinking. The more self-aware they are, the more chance they have of achieving a certain measure of freedom. Freedom for a human being consists in knowing the extent to which he is conditioned, and choosing his course accordingly. But there is at every point a limitation upon our choice. Marx says here : 'Men make their own history, but they make it not of their own accord or under self-chosen conditions, but under given and transmitted conditions. The tradition of all dead generations weighs like a mountain on the brain of the living.'

Marx's point could do with some amplification. He means that individuals think of themselves and their ideas as the initiators of action, instead of being mere agents or rather the channels through which it came about. A seventeenth-century Puritan thought that the Puritan revolution came about because the King and his followers were wicked malignants upon whom the Lord's elect were executing justice. The illustration is not quite exact, because in the idea of the 'Lord's elect' there is an element of determinism, and the Puritans did think of themselves as channels of a higher power operating through them. That was mere human egoism of the usual sort, which meant by God themselves and their own cause writ large. They would have no idea of the underlying economic and social forces in the age which bore them upward like a tide to success, and which were the real determining factors in their victory. Only a very rare and independent cross-bench mind would have seen that. James Harington in fact did ; but then he was a doctrinaire Republican, whose independent intellect fascinated and solaced the King who chose him for company in the last months of his life. Neither side liked Harington ; he understood too much for them ; he saw through the pretences of both sides ; he saw that it was all pretty much self-interest. He was a man

outside ordinary human action. He is often spoken of nowadays
as a precursor of Marx. As if that were his only claim to attention! His mind was a mind of original power and interest
in and for itself.

Marx regarded technical inventions in the sphere of production as a most important agent of social change, as having something like the importance of selection by adaptation in natural
science. He says in a note to *Capital*:

A critical history of technology would show how little any of
the inventions of the eighteenth century are the work of a single
individual. Hitherto there has been no such book. Darwin has
interested us in the history of Nature's technology, i.e. in the
formation of the organs of plants and animals, which organs serve
as instruments of production for sustaining life. Does not the history
of the productive organs of man, of organs that are the material
basis of all social organisation, deserve equal attention? And would
not such a history be easier to compile, since, as Vico says, human
history differs from natural history in this, that we have made the
former but not the latter? Technology discloses man's mode of
dealing with Nature – the process of production by which he sustains
his life, and thereby also lays bare the mode of formation of his
social relations, and of the mental conceptions that flow from them.
Every history of religion, even that which fails to take account of
this material basis, is uncritical. It is, in reality, much easier to
discover by analysis the earthly core of the misty creations of
religion, than it is, conversely, to develop from the actual relations
of life the corresponding celestialised forms of those relations.

I should interpolate here that these latter are the work of imagination, of the unconscious, and not intellectual constructs at
all; compare the medievals' belief in the angelic hierarchy that
came to reflect for them the feudal hierarchy of life on earth.
This was not consciously thought out; that was its strength, its
roots were in the life of imagination and belief. Only a ration-
alist like Marx would expect to arrive at it by thinking. 'The
latter is the only materialistic, and therefore the only scientific, method.' He means, to proceed from the external objective
world to the inner world of mind. 'The weak points in the abstract materialism of natural science, a materialism that ex-
cludes history and its process, are at once evident from the

abstract and ideological conceptions of its spokesmen, whenever they venture beyond the bounds of their own speciality.' A shrewd hit that, which has not lost its point in an age that has paid too much attention to the commonplaces of Jeans and Eddington and such mystically-minded popularizers of science.

What we can see here is that Marx did not think of man as a passive agent. He insisted that man makes his own history, but within certain conditions limiting his action. Can we say to the extent of determining that history? Up to a point, yes ; or perhaps we should say, beyond a certain point. Let us take an illustration. We might say that if certain events had not taken place in our history – if Richard II had not been defeated and dethroned, if Edward IV had lived or Edward VI or Henry, Prince of Wales, if Queen Anne had had a son to succeed her – the whole surface pattern of our history would have been different ; and yet it is probable that the underlying story of England would have been much the same, its fortune not so very different, for that depends upon more profound forces at work – its geographical position and character, the economic endowment of the island, nature of the people, their social structure and so on. There is the issue, simply stated. The point is whether we mean by history the surface story, which is capable of infinite variation, or the underlying story which is profoundly conditioned.*

I do not know whether this distinction has been made use of before ; and yet it is for lack of it that there has been endless discussion, largely due to this confusion. Everybody is bound to recognize that there is illimitable possibility of variation in the surface events of history – or almost illimitable ; but also everybody is bound to recognize that the fundamental story of a country – say, what it can do or not – is largely conditioned for it. For example, in the modern industrial age it has been

* The American reader may work out for himself, as an exercise, a comparable series of changes and chances, of ifs and buts, in regard to the civil war. Yet one cannot but think that the underlying configuration of historic forces in the United States in the nineteenth century would have worked out much the same as it did.

impossible for Italy, for all her efforts, to be a great power; she has not the natural resources. The efforts were therefore senseless; they went against the sense of history, and she was bound to be pulled back by that necessity.

This historical point of view has a decisive importance for politics. Constantly in human history we see some power inflating itself beyond what its real resources can stand, and then it gets brought back again to normal – i.e. what is in correspondence with its real resources – usually by way of catastrophe and defeat. In the modern world we have seen it happen in the sixteenth and seventeenth centuries with Spain, which overexerted itself to dominate Europe and so brought on a decline that has lasted ever since. France under Louis XIV inflated herself beyond what she could really carry – and underwent defeat and much suffering. Again under the impact of the revolution and the leadership of Napoleon she took the opportunity of the divisions among the other European powers to establish a domination over Europe. In the nature of things it could not last. Why should anybody try – and bring on themselves such catastrophes? And yet in our time Germany has made two attempts – bringing what disaster upon herself in the process! Her success could only in the nature of things be temporary: it could last only so long as Europe was disunited and divided in resistance to her. She was not really strong enough to dominate the whole Western world, any more than Japan was to rule the whole of the East. Why should people attempt the impossible?

The answer is that they do not know the conditions that determine what they can do; they have no historical understanding. 'Things and actions are what they are, and the consequences of them will be what they will be: why then should we desire to be deceived?' Such was the ultimate wisdom of a philosopher among theologians, Bishop Butler.

This opens up further problems. If people understood how their action was limited and conditioned, would they act at all? Too much knowledge is a discouragement to action. So much of human action is senseless, wasteful, purposeless. Without a large penumbra of irrationality, of bravado, of attempting the impossible, of embarking upon forlorn hopes, it might be difficult for human beings to get going at all. Such is the nature of human nature. And in an age which has ceased to devote its serious mental efforts to analysing the nature of God, what we are up against is the nature of man. In so far as men are discouraged from effort, or withdraw (so far as possible) from active participation in events, the pattern is changed. One can go no further here. What we can say, on the practical side, is that people could do with a great deal more of historical understanding than they have got. Just a little more understanding of history would prevent them making quite such fools of themselves or bringing down upon their heads, upon intelligent as well as unintelligent, the catastrophes, the disasters, the suffering they do.

The point I was making was this : that it depends whether you mean by history the surface stream of events, in which case you belong to the free-will school of thought, or whether you mean by it the deep underlying tides and currents, in which case you are apt to be a determinist. These two schools of thought, then, are not mutually exclusive and contradictory ; we discover how pointless much of the historical controversy between one side and the other has been – all for lack of distinguishing what each side really had in mind.

Marx had nothing to say on this, because he did not arrive at the distinction. He left his view of history undeveloped and fragmentary. His historical sense forbade him to commit himself to any development of his theory which was contradictory to how things come about in practice. ('At any rate I am not a Marxist,' he declared at the end of his life.) So he indicated what his view was rather sketchily in the passages I have quoted, left it at that, and spent the remainder of his life applying it and carrying it out in economics and politics, in both theory and practice. Nevertheless his view of history was at the heart of all his work and action. After his death, Engels, by way of countering extreme interpretations, attempted to explain what Marx and he had meant. He said that they had not meant to claim an absolute supremacy for economic considerations over all other factors ; that the actual form of social organization is often moulded by political, legal, philosophical or religious doctrines. 'It is not that the economic situation is the cause, in the sense of being the only active agent, and that everything else is only a passive result. It is, on the contrary, a case of mutual action on the basis of the economic necessity, which in the last instance always works itself out.'

The position may be put like this. On the basis of the physical environment, geographical and economic, man acts. He makes his social environment, though its character will be determined in the last resort by the physical environment, which for the most part it is not possible for man to transcend, though he may in some degree transform it. On that basis, out of the mutual action and interaction, of an increasingly complex kind as society develops, other modes of man's social life are formed, religious and cultural, intellectual and aesthetic. But there will always remain a continuing element of the original physical environment that is not transcended – one can't jump off the planet or even the island – and this remains a conditioning factor all through the subsequent processes of man's history. That is all.

We may distinguish two main phases in the development of the Marxist attitude to history – with the importance that that has had for communism in contemporary world-politics. In the first phase the emphasis was all on the importance of conditions ; we may call it the deterministic phase. In the second, the emphasis has been all on man as the active agent in the historical process : the dialectical phase. It is all very natural and explicable. In the earlier period the Marxists were themselves under the pressure of social conditions, the objects of action ; only with the Russian revolution did they come to be able to mould conditions, to become the active agents of historic change. They found the latter altogether more agreeable ; as Lenin wrote in the preface to *The State and Revolution*, which he had not time to finish : 'It is more pleasant and more useful to undergo the experience of revolution than to write about it.' (At least, we may agree, for those who come out on top ; but for the others, even those who helped to make the revolution : Bukharin, Radek, Zinoviev, Kamenev, Rykov, Smirnov? – the list of the liquidated prolongs itself indefinitely.) Anyhow,

the change has been reflected in a marked change of emphasis
in the theory.

What is the relation between man, the agent, and the environment? I have indicated what Marx and Engels thought about it
in the previous pages. The process of action and interaction between one and the other they conceived of in terms of Hegel's
dialectic. This may be described simply as Hegel's way of thinking of evolution in the realm of ideas : you take any proposition
as your *thesis* ; the reverse gives you its *antithesis* ; the conflict
between the two and its outcome, reconciling something of
each in a new proposition, give you the *synthesis*. *Schluss*! Be-
hold the rabbit out of the hat! Such is the famous Hegelian
triad. I fear nothing is more boring in modern thought – or few
things more boring ; and nothing has been more disastrous to
Marxism than its attachment to the Hegelian dialectic. Perhaps
the dialectic had some use for its time : it provided a scheme
within which the evolutionary process could be grasped conveniently, and one that was rather more subtle than a uni-
formly progressive development – it allowed for setbacks and
reverses in the process, along with leaps ahead. It did not err
on the side of 'the inevitability of gradualness'. (The Fabians,
being English, escaped the influence of both Hegel and Marx ;
they were Darwinians.) What Marx did was to take over the
conception of dialectical process from Hegel, who had used it
to explain the development of ideas, and apply it to the world
of actual events, in short to history.

That was all very well for its day. But that day was precisely
a hundred years ago. It is time that the Marxists, like everybody
else, did a little fresh thinking. True, most people have not got
up to the point of knowing what all the fuss over Marxism is
about. Marxism is certainly plumb in the middle of the intellectual issues of our time, but we want to be able to improve
on it, pass beyond it.

And this is what is wrong with the Marxist dialectic of history. In the first place it is an intellectual formula that is applied from outside to the rich diversity, the almost infinite
variability of history ; it does not arise from the phenomena,
the facts themselves ; it is a piece of *appliqué* work. That is in

itself a grave defect. Any theory of history, to be at all satisfactory, must arise from the nature of the material. The same holds good for science. In the breakdown of the transcendent claims of metaphysics there is considerable agreement that the best way to advance knowledge is for the separate disciplines, on the basis of their specialist information, to reach forward to the general and the abstract; rather than for the general and the abstract to impose their assumptions and preconceptions upon the more assured knowledge of the sciences, natural or social. The imposition of the dialectic upon history is an obvious relic of the old transcendent claims of idealist metaphysics: and it is in contradiction to the implications of Marxism as an essentially historical doctrine.

It is far too schematic, too rigid a formula for the subtlety of history, where peoples and causes are not only defeated and fall out of the process, but sometimes suffer, almost inexplicably, a failure of nerve and disappear. It is insufficiently supple or flexible for the infinite variety of historical phenomena, with all the ups and downs, the ebbs and flows and the innumerable coiled convolutions of human action within those processes that are determinable. Better to have a wise and wary scepticism than to rivet such an iron framework upon such refractory material. Better to have no theory at all and trust to common sense in the English fashion than to sacrifice truth to a false theory. Actually there is no reason to be driven to scepticism; I have done my best to build up a theory that is in correspondence with the facts, and any theory of history must be one that arises from the phenomena.

Far worse is the practical consequence of the Marxist dialectic; it gives you no objective standard as to the sense or rationality of action. It becomes in practice a dangerous pragmatism – all the more dangerous because so ineffective, as well as misleading. That this was so may be proved by the senseless, as well as unscrupulous, record of communist international policy between the two wars. The communists made it their main end and aim to destroy social democracy, on the assumption that it would be communism that would emerge triumphant. Capitalism being the *thesis*, social democracy the *antithesis*, communism must then be the *synthesis*, the outcome of the conflict : so ran the argument. Could anything be more childish? One can always arrange the triad according to what one wants to obtain from it, like manipulating the oracle. One might as well take social democracy as the thesis, communism the antithesis, fascism the synthesis ; which was in fact nearer to what then came about. Throughout the period of the Weimar Republic the communists made it their main end and aim to undermine it, and directed their chief attack against the social democrats who supported it. The result was not victory for the communists, but for the nazis. I am not saying that other people were not to blame too, but the upshot of these lunatic efforts was that millions of simple good men died in the event. How often in these years one has thought of the cry of Shaw's St Joan : 'Must then a Christ perish in torment in every age to save those that have no imagination?' I do not go so far as to expect human beings to have much imagination ; I merely ask for a little common sense, and a little historical understanding from those who set themselves up to be their leaders.

The plain fact is that the dialectic left its adherents with no standards of right and wrong in action, of what made sense and what did not make sense – except what was to the interest of Russia. A war, which in truth was waged in defence of civilization, was an imperialist war until the very morning of Hitler's attack on Russia, when it became in that moment a just and right war in defence of democracy. To such bankruptcy had years of deliberate confusion of means with ends brought the communists. It was a terrible degradation of any standards of historical judgement, at least as bad as that of those people in Britain who thought it possible to come to terms with the nazis. That too was always nonsense and showed no understanding of history or any political sense ; but the communists were sinning against the supposed light. A simpler point of view than mine, or theirs, would condemn their behaviour as morally wrong, indeed criminal. But our business is with historical judgement here, not with ethics. And I content myself with saying that their whole record in that period did not make sense historically. In history the proof of the pudding is in the eating.

But one ought not to need ten or twenty years to tell what it is going to be. Anyone with a good knowledge of history and a common-sense judgement of how human affairs proceed could have told beforehand how fatal this course of action would be.

I am not blaming all this upon Marxism as a body of thought, still less upon historical materialism as sketched by Marx and Engels, but upon the narrow and sharpened 'dialectical material-ism' that was developed from Lenin onwards. The historical outlook of Marx and Engels was a much wider and more catholic thing than the orthodoxy of their communist followers. Here we are only concerned with its influence on the conception of history and historical writing. As such, taken at its broad-est and best, it has had a stimulating and fruitful influence – immense on the continent, and even at last beginning to show signs in England. One can go so far as to say that to be a good historian in our time one needs to have been something of a Marxist. One needs to know what it is all about, to have seen the point of it, to have felt the influence – even if one comes out the other side. Croce came out the other side, but he had undergone something of the influence of Marx, though still more that of Hegel. Apart from orthodox Marxists, one can see the influence at work with such eminent historians as Ros-tovtzeff and Vinogradoff; in Britain, with R. H. Tawney, Sir George Clark, and A. H. M. Jones, the distinguished ancient-historian.

Marxism, like any other form of evolutionary thought, brings us up against the question of historical relativism, or historicism (*Historismus*). This is the problem that lies at the heart of his-torical thinking, and to which the most eminent minds of our time in this field have addressed themselves, Dilthey, Troeltsch, Croce – I cannot think altogether satisfactorily.

We had an example of the way the problem opens up when we mentioned the change of emphasis in Marxist thought from determinism to activisim with Lenin and the Russian re-volution. It is a good example of the way theory adapts itself to new needs, changed conditions. But what is true? Is there any way of arriving at a view that is true for all conditions? Are we not reduced to a purely pragmatic attitude to truth? – you change your view of what is true according to your needs.

That is the intellectual problem, I had almost said disease, of our time. One can see its ravages on all hands in the confusion of the communists between means and ends in political action, and the consequent senselessness of much of their record from the point of view of achieving even their own objectives ;* in the criminal and deliberate nihilism of the nazis, the cheap Machiavellianism of the fascists. One can see it no less in the scepticism, the Laodiceanism in action, of good men who find the problem too much for them and give up any endeavour to bring an ordered body of thought out of the welter of contemporary experience. Others think to stay the ravages of contemporary relativism – the decline of belief in absolute standards, the psychological undermining and questioning of all motives and so on – by a crude reassertion of the very doctrines, religious or metaphysical, that have been found wanting. That is no way to help us. We have to accept the new and more profound knowledge our time has brought us, with the new and deeper doubts – and surmount them ; if possible achieve a synthesis.

Let us look at how the problem struck a few choice spirits. Burckhardt, the historian of culture, was one of the first to sense it.

History is actually the most unscientific of all the sciences although it communicates so much that is worth knowing. Clear-cut concepts belong to logic, not to history, where everything is in a state of flux, of perpetual transition and combination. Philosophical and historical ideas differ in essence and origin; the former must be as firm and exclusive as possible, the latter as fluid and open.... Nothing wholly unconditioned has ever existed, and nothing that was solely a determinant. At the same time, one element predominates in one aspect of life, another in another. It is all a question of relative importance, of the dominant at any particular time.

Burckhardt did not go any further than that ; the tendency of

* In Russia since the death of Stalin one observes the convulsive attempts to recover from the ravages of Stalinism. But the dead are dead – in millions.

his mind was sceptical, though full of ripe reflections. A practical deduction that he drew was that in judging the men of a particular epoch with their virtues and vices we must see them 'within the system of their time'. It is a part of the historic sense to be able to judge an age in relation to its needs, its problems and achievements, to set its failures against the satisfactions given. But he did not go further to draw any implications other than this limited practical one.

Morley did, towards the end of his life, in an interesting lecture, *Notes on Politics and History*. After describing what he calls 'the historic method' he says :

It is easy to see that the ascendancy of the historic method has its drawbacks. Study of all the successive stages in beliefs, institutions, forms of art, only too soon grows into a substitute for direct criticism of all these things upon their merits and in themselves. Inquiry what the event actually was and what its significance and interpretation becomes secondary to inquiry how it came about. Too exclusive attention to dynamic aspects weakens the energetic duties of the static. More than one school has thus seen the predominance of historic-mindedness excessive. It means, they truly say, in its very essence, veto of the absolute, persistent substitution of the relative. Your method is non-moral like any other scientific instrument. There is no more conscience in your comparative history than there is in comparative anatomy.... Talk of 'eternal political truths', or 'first principles of government', has no meaning. Stated summarily, is not your history one prolonged 'becoming' (*fieri*, *werden*), an endless sequence of action, reaction, generation, destruction, renovation, 'a tale of sound and fury signifying nothing'. Such argument as this, I know, may be hard pressed, and it is in truth a protest for the absolute that cannot be spared to many active causes. But that relative tests and standards are the keys both to real knowledge of history, and to fair measure of its actors, is a doctrine not likely to lose its hold.

In short Morley knew what the argument was about, and funked it.

Dilthey realized all its implications and formulated his answer. Professor Hodges, in a summary of Dilthey's position, says :

This widening of consciousness through historical knowledge has disconcerting results. Every age expresses its attitude to life and the world in certain principles of thought and conduct, which are regarded in that age as absolute and unconditionally valid.... The historian discovers these principles in every age which he studies, but also discerns that they vary from age to age, and that, in spite of the claim to absoluteness which is always made, changed circumstances always result in changed principles, which are therefore historically relative ... History, having recorded the relativity of all ideas and practices, points to its own relativity, and leaves us in the position known as historicism, or historical relativism. Dilthey recognises this, and there is evidence that he was visited by occasional twinges of nervousness at the blank prospect which it opens up – a prospect which has led many in the present age to cynicism and apathy, and caused others to seek escape in dogmatic obscurantism and authoritarianism. There are some, however, who have found it possible to look historicism in the face and yet avoid discouragement, and in spite of occasional doubts, Dilthey was one of these. He not merely admits the necessity of historicism, he proclaims it and regards it as a source of freedom and inspiration.

How can he do this? Because he sees historicism first of all as a deliverance from superstition and illusion, and secondly as a revelation of the manifold capacities of human life. If our grandfathers reacted to their situation in one way and we react to ours in another, the conclusion which Dilthey draws is not that no one can ever know how to act or think, but that in every situation man can find a way..., And the more we learn that every particular set of principles is the mind's reaction to a particular set of circumstances, the more it appears that even historicism has to admit one absolute after all, viz. the marvellously adaptable human mind itself.

It will hardly escape attention that this, though very interesting and suggestive in itself – and though we may agree with it – is not a satisfactory answer. It is an answer on the practical plane ; it tells us something of the uses of historical thinking, but does not tell us how far its categories are valid – whether what it tells us is true.

Croce tells us that 'historicism (the science of history), scientifically speaking, is the affirmation that life and reality are history and history alone. The necessary corollary to this affirmation is the negation of the theory which holds that reality can be divided into super-history and history, into a world of ideas and values and a lower world which reflects them.' He means that events and ideas are all part of the flux of history. 'The quick of this argument lies in the demonstration that the ideas or the values which have been taken as the measure and the models of history are not universal ideas and values but are themselves particular and historical facts elevated to the rank of universals.' Here again we observe the sceptical note that proceeds from all who are affected by historical relativism. Croce is quite right when he says that the historical outlook completely undermines a superficial rationalism, of the eighteenth- and nineteenth-century type, and in its place develops a more profound rationalism, which, realizing how irrational men and events are, would on the basis of that knowledge the more satisfactorily take some control and shape them into order. Leadership of the irrational by the rational is the end, not the old superficial denial of irrationality ; its discovery, or at any rate the discovery of its preposterous extent, by modern psychology should be a powerful aid to its enlistment in the service of reason and sense ; indeed, it is a necessary condition. It is that aspect of the extension of knowledge in our time that gives us most hope.

Croce, who has spent a good deal of his life in philosophizing and has written many large works on the subject, now aligns himself with those who see no place for metaphysics. 'The conclusion that philosophy serves no other purpose than as a "methodology of historical thought" has often been formulated and doctrinally demonstrated by me to the great displeasure of the so-called pure philosophers.' In the belief that philosophy is merely good sense, he asks 'whether there is anything else to be known in the world other than the events among which we live and have to work, and whether philosophical reflections can ever be justified as anything but a way or method by which to achieve this sole effective and useful knowledge'. In fact, he has already told us in a chapter entitled 'Historical Knowledge Considered as Complete Knowledge' : 'It is not enough to say that history is historical judgment, it is necessary to add that every judgment is an historical judgment or, quite simply, history. . . . Historical judgment is not a variety of knowledge, but it is

knowledge itself; it is the form which completely fills and ex-
hausts the field of knowing, leaving no room for anything else.'

Now we know where Croce's disciple, Collingwood, got the
conclusion of *The Idea of Nature* from. He is arguing that scientific work is in essence historical.

The scientist who wishes to know that such an event has taken
place in the world of nature can know this only by consulting the
record left by the observer and interpreting it, subject to certain
rules, in such a way as to satisfy himself that the man whose work
it records really did observe what he professes to have observed.
This consultation and interpretation of records is the characteristic
feature of historical work. Every scientist who says that Newton
observed the effect of a prism on sunlight, or that Adams saw
Neptune, or that Pasteur observed that grape-juice played upon by
air to a certain temperature underwent no fermentation, is talking
history. The facts first observed by Newton, Adams and Pasteur have
since then been observed by others, but every scientist who says
that light is split up by the prism or that Neptune exists or that
fermentation is prevented by a certain degree of heat is still talking
history: he is talking about the whole class of historical facts which
are occasions on which someone has made these observations. Thus
a 'scientific' fact is a class of historical facts; and no one can
understand what a scientific fact is unless he understands enough
about the theory of history to understand what an historical fact
is ...
I conclude that natural science as a form of thought exists and
always has existed in a context of history and depends on historical
thought for its existence. From this I venture to infer that no one
can understand natural science unless he understands history: and
that no one can answer the question what nature is unless he knows
what history is. This is a question which Alexander and Whitehead
have not asked. And that is why I answer the question 'Where do
we go from here?' by saying, 'We go from the idea of nature to
the idea of history.'

At that point Collingwood died. It is difficult to see how he
could have gone any further. It is also remarkable how obtuse
clever men can be. Of course, in a sense history underlies everything. It is obvious that everything has an historical aspect. But
that does not mean that history *is* everything. And there is

surely a plain confusion of thought beneath what Collingwood says. The real essence of scientific investigation is not the 'consultation and interpretation of records', as in history; it is in verification by experiment. There is an analogous 'verification by experiment' in history, where, as I have said, the proof of the pudding is in the eating. But this is *ex post facto*; you cannot test it out beforehand, there are too many imponderables in the equation.

It seems to me that Croce and Collingwood land themselves in a historical mysticism as dangerous as any pragmatism – dangerous because it does not distinguish between things. Croce identifies the judgement of events with the knowledge of their genesis: 'the concept that concrete and true knowledge is always historical knowledge has the obvious consequence that the knowledge or qualification or judgment of an event cannot be separated or distinguished from the knowledge of its genesis.' But origin is not the same thing as validity, nor is knowledge of the origin the same thing as judgement of it. Croce goes too far in his *mystique de l'histoire* when he tells us: 'Reality is history and is only historically known. The sciences certainly measure it and classify it as is necessary, but properly speaking do not know it, nor is it their business to know its intrinsic nature.' He ends by identifying humanism with the historical outlook. 'The heir of this great labour is historicism, which contains in itself liberation from transcendence of all kinds, affirmation of moral, political and economic life, emphasis upon passion and poetry, rejuvenation of intellectual and moral life, dialectic which is its new logical instrument.'

We may agree with Croce that historical thinking liberates us from the transcendental, and with his polemic against the wholesale intrusion of ethical judgements from one age and clime into totally different ones. 'Those who on the plea of narrating history bustle about as judges, condemning here and giving absolution there, because they think that this is the office of history, are generally recognised as devoid of historical sense.' This gives short shift to Acton with his famous dictum, 'Power tends to corrupt, and absolute power corrupts absolutely.' And indeed it is too simple and summary: the code of a high-minded Victorian gentleman applied to the welter of history. But does that mean that one can apply no ethical standards to history? I think not. Very well, what standards are there? Croce gives us a hint in a passage which contradicts much of what he has said before, when he says, 'Since every affirmation is a judgment, and judgment implies category, the constitutive element of historiography is the system of judgement-categories.'

We have seen that if you follow the principle of dialectic you have no external standards of judgement at all, they are one with the process. My view of this difficult question is as follows. The standards or categories must arise from the nature of the phenomena we are studying, whether historical or scientific. They form something of a system in accordance with the experience of life and in accordance with their own logical coherence, by both of which they must be tested all the time, constantly. Standards which can be applied to history, which are appropriate to history, arise therefore out of history. Many courses of action condemn themselves, and not only by disaster or failure; they may be criminal or immoral. Such judgements are possible, as I hope to show immediately. Many men in history condemn themselves, or conversely are to be admired and praised. Of course we must understand them and *their* standards in terms of their age and *its* standards. But are those standards or values completely transcended by time? They certainly have a time-element in them, and the time-element is greater in, say, political and ethical standards than it is in aesthetic or purely intellectual – in mathematics or pure logic for example. One might almost construct a hierarchy of values, from those which are most subject to changing conditions to those which are least.

When we look into these standards we see that they have not only an element that comes from the changing conditions of the time, but also a more permanent element which relates to something continuous and enduring. Let us take a Greek tragedy: a good deal of it reflects the social conditions of a vanished age, its standards of judgement; but enclosed within that envelope there are aesthetic values that speak to us for all time

– or at any rate so long as man is recognizably man. There are things of beauty – and probably as Burckhardt and many others have thought (Robert Bridges and James Joyce among them) aesthetic values are more constant than any – that come across to us still with undiminished force. But it would not be common sense to deny that there are other values that come across to us too with authority and command our assent – ethical values. For the plain fact is that underlying all the flux and change of history, the mutually contradictory claims of religions, the parochial squabbles of the sects for our allegiance, the indisputable tendency of individual egoism to assert itself as universal – underneath all the change of circumstances and condition there is a certain continuum to which all standards may be related for their validity: the nature of man *qua man*. It is that that gives substance, a real basis to our moral judgements, however conditioned by time, so that we may as historians condemn Nero for a bad man and acclaim Jesus as a good man.

A modern philosopher, Professor Stebbing, says:

Even if ethical principles are eternal and immutable it is certain that they need to be re-interpreted for every period and re-thought for every generation. Our moral beliefs, our standards of right and wrong, our conception of our relations to other men undergo some change as our modes of living change.

She tells us that it is a mistake to deduce morals from metaphysics; that

morality is not to be deduced from anything else; the concept of moral obligation is not to be exhibited as a deduction from a system of the universe. On the contrary, the fact that we know what it is to be morally obliged is a datum that must be fitted in, if we are so ambitious as to construct a theory of the universe.

All this fits in, from the side of a contemporary philosopher, with the knowledge that accrues to us from history and historical method. We are not left with a complete scepticism about everything, as the result of our experience of historical relativism. We *can* build up a body of knowledge, from which we can tell, for example, in one sphere that it was always nonsense to try to appease the Nazis – it was contrary to the nature of a régime whose whole inner logic was aggression and conquest; or again, to hold that there can be a future for the Liberal party in Britain when its whole social and economic foundation has given way. Historical thinking can tell you both these things; or to take an example from a different sphere: that the Christian doctrine of love among men is a better basis for human relations in a society than envy and hatred. And that without subscribing to any metaphysical propositions of a quite incredible kind.

This body of knowledge that we build up out of history does relate to the needs and times we live in; and of course there must be a constant process of adaptation of knowledge to the time. A great deal of earlier knowledge is constantly being rendered out of date, like much of early science, astrology, alchemy – having served its purpose in developing astronomy and chemistry – or for that matter theology or political and economic thought. But we draw out of it all that which we need, that which lasts, stands the longer tests of time and relates to the enduring continuum of man's experience as man. The way to truth then is to understand these changes in accordance with changing conditions, to pierce through to the underlying continuity of knowledge and experience. Historical thinking is the appropriate method. For knowledge too has its own continuum no less than experience; it is not merely pragmatic, yielding temporary answers to temporary questions, nor merely utilitarian, to be discarded out of mind. It may be forgotten – and come up again after centuries. It is perpetually being remade and remoulded to our needs, of which some are practical, others intellectual, such as the universal human need to get coherence out of what we think, reduce to rational order what we experience.

However relativist the historian, he can then agree with the philosopher that there is positive knowledge: 'It is an illusion to find the value of our lives here and now in a life to come; it is an illusion to suppose that nothing is worth while for me unless I live for ever; it is an illusion to suppose that there is no uncompensated loss, no sacrifice that is without requital, no grief that is unassuaged. But it is also no illusion but uncontested fact that here and now we know that hatred, cruelty, intolerance, and indifference to human misery are evil; that love, kindliness, tolerance, forgiveness, and truth are good, so unquestionably good that we do not need God or heaven to assure us of their worth.'*

No; those values emerge from, and rest upon, the positive experience of man in history.

*L. Susan Stebbing, *Ideals and Illusions*.

6 History and Education

It is evident that history is a subject of great educational value. At the universities it has become the leading arts subject. I agree with Trevelyan's general judgement:

The older I get and the more I observe the tendencies and conditions of our latter day, the more certain I become that history must be the basis of humane (that is, non-scientific) education in the future. Without some knowledge of history other doors will remain locked. For example, the reading of poetry and prose literature, other than current books, must rest on some knowledge of the times past when the older books were written. Some understanding of the social and political scene of Chaucer's, Shakespeare's, Milton's, Swift's world, of the world of Boswell, of Wordsworth and Shelley and Byron, of Dickens and of Trollope, of Carlyle and Ruskin, is necessary in order fully to appreciate the works in question, or even in some cases to understand what they are about. Music needs no such historic introduction to be fully appreciated, for it is not allusive, or only slightly. But literature is allusive, each book rooted in the soil of the time when it was written. Unless our great English literature is to become a sealed book to the English people (as indeed I fear it is to many) our countrymen must know something of times past.

That is already a strong case, but I think the case is stronger still. There is nothing that gives unity to all the other arts subjects so much as history. So many of them spring out of it, or find much of their material there – such subjects as anthropology and sociology, economics and law, to a lesser extent languages. All of them have their historical aspect and meet together in history. It is a subject above all catholic, capacious, mixed; not a pure subject like mathematics, music or logic; it is as wide and various as life. Nor does it only provide the best common meeting-ground for all the separate arts disciplines; it gives them the best and most fruitful junction with the natural sciences.

Let me illustrate what I am trying to say. Suppose you are a student of a foreign language and literature. You are bound to know something of the history of the people, if you are to understand their literature; and the development of the language will lead you back again to their history, which to some extent it reflects. If you are a student of anthropology or sociology, comparative law or ethics, you will derive much of your material from the history of different peoples; without an historical sense, telling you where it comes in their development and what the circumstances are, you will not interpret it aright. The sociological circumstances of a given time and people will find expression in their literature; the dominant ethical code in their law and legislation. In each case the common ground is the history of that people and time, of which each shows a different aspect and to which they all contribute. The same holds good for the sciences and their relation to the arts. The development of science is intimately connected with the philosophical thought of its time no less than with its practical needs. Early astronomy developed in response to the demands of religious observance as well as the needs of travel by land and sea; navigation and commerce have given rise to much scientific discovery; geometry arose from the necessity for land-measurement. The student of geography will find that his subject goes hand in hand with geology on one side and history on the other. The study of geographical exploration is as much history as it is geography. Some of the classics of science are also classics of literature, for example, Bacon, Galileo, the works of Darwin and Huxley. Such arts as architecture and music have a scientific aspect; the story of their technical developments is a part of history. One can study the evolution of instruments: the pianoforte from the harpsichord and so from the virginals, the violin from the viol and the lute. And there is the whole historical approach to science itself; the men who made the achievements of science were men of their time, conditioned by the intellectual and social interests and character of their time. One recalls that the greatest statesman of Greek antiquity, Pericles, was a close friend of the scientist Anaxagoras ; the poet Euripides was another of his friends. In fact the cross-contacts and affiliations in the realm of knowledge are infinitely valuable and fertilizing. But they all have their earth-bed in history, so to say, if this is not too passive a metaphor for a subject which operates more as a galvanic conductor, or a stream of connective energy in its own right.

From the time of the Renaissance up to our own time the Classics and the Bible occupied the centre of the field in humane studies and operated as the chief unifying influence in education. This was roughly true all over Europe (except for Russia and the Balkans), and it had a deep effect in making a common European mind among the educated classes, in spite of national and religious divisions. Educated men had Plato and Aristotle, the Greek tragedians and historians, Virgil and Horace, Plutarch, Livy, Tacitus, the literature and history of the Bible, as a common background all over the Western world. It remained in full force in education in this country up to the last generation.

In the almost complete breakdown of the older classical education in our time, where are we to look for a unifying influence to take its place? Where indeed but in history can our common experience and the different humane studies meet? There is no other possible competitor, and this is the chief practical suggestion I have to make, the message of this book.

It might be argued that history is a disunifying influence rather than a unifying one ; that nations would be still further fortified in their own national traditions and not look beyond their boundaries to a European or a world community.

It is true that the mental world of the average man is that of his own country and its language and literature. But increasingly today, with newspapers, wireless and films, he is enabled to form some picture, if a partial and uneven one, of other countries. Most English people have an infinitely better idea of America than of any other country, of the States three thousand miles away than they have of their next-door neighbour, France. It is precisely in so far as people are educated that they become more aware and more capable of understanding other nations

and their traditions. The man who has a good historical education is not confined to one country's view of its own past; the
educated Englishman does not share George III's view of the
American revolution, any more than the educated American
looks at it through the eyes of John Hancock or John Adams.
As our historical reading widens and our judgement of events
matures, we find great achievements and sad mistakes and much
humdrum endurance everywhere in the human record; and we
come to see all the histories of different peoples, with their con-
tacts of peace and war, their currents of mutual influence and
reaction, their parallels and affiliations, their similarities and
contrasts, all as part of one history. Arrived at that view-point,
history is the most synoptic and unifying of all studies. But it
implies, and demands, education; fortunately also it provides
it. The process is a dual one.

One of the main advantages of history in education is that
the subject grows with one from a very elementary stage to the
last refinements of ripe maturity and sceptical wisdom. The
subject is capable of appealing to quite young children, as I
remember in my own case and have described in *A Cornish
Childhood*: how a great-aunt of mine had a history book (there
were no books in our house); it must have been a squalid text-
book of a hot Protestant character, but I was fascinated by what
it said about Mary Tudor and passionately enraged against her.
This must have been at about the age of six. History is certainly
capable of arousing the passions. This is no very dangerous
thing, perhaps, at the age of six, and all to the good since it
awakens interest. The sedate Dr. Keatinge in a useful little book,
Studies in the Teaching of History, tells us:

It is as an introduction to the world of human nature that history
is chiefly to be prized. If stress is laid on the biographical side, history
is a panorama of character in action in every conceivable situation,
it widens indefinitely the circle of our acquaintances, it provides
abundant material for the analysis of motive, it gives opportunity
for cultivating restraint in the admiration of pleasant personalities
and charity in the judgment of unpleasant ones.

And that is about right. Children are interested in personalities and their stories; they have a shrewd sense of character,

which is developed by learning about persons in history and how they behave ; after all it is only an extension of the living world they inhabit, with this added advantage – that they can see how things turned out with them ; it gives them a basis for reflection. They do not inhabit a world of atoms and molecules, protons and electrons, chemical substances and atomic numbers – at least these do not form their personal acquaintance whom they have to learn to get on with in life. And though it may be said that the essential business of learning to get on with other human beings, to know them and understand them and judge their nature, is to be learned in the commerce of life itself, yet that same life portrayed pictorially, unrolled before our eyes in history, is a valuable extension of life and a vast aid to our reflecting upon it. It is true, alas, that most people learn very little anyway ; but that is no argument against what they might learn if they set themselves about it. Dr Keatinge states an extremely strong case for the study of history in schools even on purely utilitarian grounds :

Most schools of any importance have a science laboratory, upon which a considerable sum of money is spent yearly; for the history lesson few schools supply any apparatus but a text-book and a black-board. Natural science, as a branch of knowledge equipped with methods and apparatus, has had the start of social science. Moreover, it appeals to the crude utilitarian instinct and, in spite of the efforts of headmasters, who know their business, the pressure of pseudo-utilitarianism is one which it is difficult to resist.

After allowing that it is desirable that all schoolboys should be introduced to the world of science and to the elements of scientific method, Dr Keatinge continues :

But once his schooldays are over, not one boy in a hundred will ever again be brought into contact with chemical processes or be compelled to make any physical calculations. The ordinary adult pays experts to perform these operations for him, and as a rule is too sensible to run the risk of doing them badly.... It is different with the other great department of school studies. The youth may never again see a test tube or a balance, but he cannot fail to be brought into contact with men.... His success in life will probably, will almost certainly, depend upon the ease and correctness with which he observes words, both written and spoken, and draws inferences from them; he will on countless occasions need to analyse documents, to abstract them, and to compare them; he will seldom be free from the necessity of inferring motives from actions and character from deeds; and it is precisely to these classes of mental operations, and to familiarity with these factors in human life, that school history, if properly conceived, and the history lesson, if properly conducted, will introduce him.

Surely everyone must agree with this out of his own experience, if he reflects on it? It is not that I am against the teaching of science in schools; it is obviously essential. But there can be too much of it, especially if it makes exclusive claims, or disconsiders the humanities. There is rather an unthinking bias in favour of science in schools nowadays; people assume that it must be the right thing, since 'This is a scientific age,' etc. and it leads obviously to certain careers in industry and elsewhere – but without reflecting whether it provides a general education for the mind. I note with interest that two enlightened science masters, Messrs Humby and James, in their book on *Science in the Schools* are inclined to doubt the value of chemistry as a school subject. I am not opposed to it in boys' schools, since a good many boys learn through their hands rather than their heads. But I doubt whether physics and chemistry have any educational value, save for a few exceptions, in girls' schools. I should have thought that in these their place might be more profitably taken, for obvious reasons, by biology, hygiene and natural history – sciences of life rather than of matter.

The expense of teaching history is inconsiderable compared with that of science, which demands more and more apparatus and laboratory equipment. The laboratory of history is the world we move about in. And it is desirable that teachers of history should be cultivated people capable of introducing their pupils to the diversity and richness, the memories and associations of the world immediately about them. What can be done may be seen from a useful little source-book compiled by the history masters at a Yorkshire school, Rothwell in the West Riding: it builds up a picture of the locality as it looked at different periods, from reliable historical sources, and thence to the wider region ; in the end one sees the history of the country depicted in the neighbourhood one knows. Every school that is any good ought to have a similar book – half-guide to the country, half-history – compiled for it.

Think of the delectable riches there are waiting to be opened up, and how fortunate we are with so varied and fertile a soil to cultivate. At once there leaps to mind the thought of the castles of Wensleydale or the Vale of Pickering – with which Sir Maurice Powicke introduces us to *Medieval England* ; the churches and manor-houses and small towns of the Cotswolds or East Anglia, the fortresses of the Welsh borders, the little sea-ports of the West Country. They all have their fascinating stories, the sediment of so many tides of life, the life of our forefathers, passing in and out of them. And what of the storied pageants of the past in the towns – Exeter, Bristol, Oxford, Norwich, Durham, York, London? They should all of them have their own source-books, the country's history as reflected in that mirror, as it actually happened in that place. An interesting job of work here, both of research and of exposition, for history teachers in schools all over the country.

It should go hand in hand with regular planned expeditions, taking history classes to the interesting things in the neighbourhood, whatever they may be – barrows, stone-circles, camps, churches, castles, sites of battles, houses of interest, neighbouring villages and towns. We can get a good idea of the chronological unfolding of the country's history from following some such order. We might even hope that as the idea spread in the country people would gradually cease to look at things of beauty with unseeing, uncaring eyes. We might even hope that they would cease to wreck and ruin the rich heritage the country got from the past, as against the infallible instinct of Philistinism for destroying what it cannot appreciate. We might even – shades of Matthew Arnold – cease to be Philistines !

All this goes along with books ; but not only with books – with plays and films, radio and television. They can all be brought into use and enjoyment, the twin themes of this book.

Take plays, for example. It is wonderful how Shakespeare can always hold the interest of a class of schoolboys. I well remember my mutinous dislike of Spenser's *Faerie Queene* – that exquisite poem, so unsuitable as a set book for boys. But not one of us disliked Shakespeare, or did not enjoy reading his plays in class ; and, as has often been observed, by the most eminent of scholars as well as by the most refractory of schoolboys, there is a great deal of English history to be learned from Shakespeare's plays. Naturally, I am still more in favour of boys and girls acting them for themselves, and being taken to see productions of them whenever there is a chance.

The same holds good of films. One of the things that gave me such satisfaction with the English film, *Henry V*, was to see a film that was not historically incongruous. It was sheer pleasure to see the lovely, coloured costumes of the late Middle Ages as they were, carefully studied from pictures and illuminated manuscripts ; to hear the music that medieval people sang, with its virile primitive harmonies ; to see the buildings, the scenes, the ships, the accoutrements as they really were. I remembered, by way of contrast, how the film of *Jane Eyre* had been ruined for me by the historical inanity of its production. As we all remember from the book, the action takes place in a sober, substantial country-house of the North Country, presumably Georgian in character. Not so in the film. Hollywood's idea of an English country-house in the early nineteenth century was donjons and battlements and corridors like a bogus-Norman Tower of London. Mr Rochester, it will be remembered, entertained a country-house party. They all came over in a coach out of the romantic period of the Wild West ; but the lady who descended from it, the *belle* of the party, was got up to look like one of the naughty ladies of the Restoration Court of Charles II. It was all absurd. It may be regarded as a disadvantage to know too much history, if it prevents one from enjoying such nonsense. But surely it would be more fun to get it right? On the other hand, a recent Hollywood production, *Judgment at Nuremberg*, qualifies as an admirable historical document. Without a single fault of taste, with justice and penetration, it exposes the responsibility of the German people for the terrible crimes done in their name against the Jews, as against other peoples.

As for the books, since history is one of the cheapest subjects to teach, costing next to nothing in equipment, schools should afford good history books and build up, what is always indispensable, a representative library. I think we can say that there has been an immense improvement both in the books and in the teaching of history in our time. The older text-books used to be deadly, guaranteed to kill any interest in the subject; the subject itself a Cinderella in most schools, and even at the universities. All that has changed. Even as a small child one can begin with fascinating books, like Eileen and Rhoda Power's *Boys and Girls of History* and *More Boys and Girls of History*; and from there go right on, with books that hold one's interest all the way along.

The royal road to appealing to the interest of the schoolboy, and not only the schoolboy, is the biographical: lives of great men, especially men of action, seamen or soldiers, adventurers, frontiersmen, pioneers, and their exciting stories; and secondly, if the two can be regarded separately, the stories themselves – the foundation of narrative history. Schoolboys respond immediately to the appeal of patriotism, to the spirit of self-devotion in such lives as Wolfe and Nelson, Robert E. Lee and Stonewall Jackson, Scott of the Antarctic, Lawrence of Arabia. They feel the thrill of achievement in such careers as Clive's or Drake's or Paul Jones's; they are capable of catching something of the greatness of spirit of such a man as Cromwell or Chatham, Lincoln or Winston Churchill. I have not forgotten the spirit of emulation that is aroused in the schoolboy, the desire to make a name in his turn, to join the ranks of those who have achieved something by which their country remembers them. I might have responded better to science if it had been presented sympathetically, through history and biography. A shortened version of Darwin's *Voyage of the Beagle*, or his *Autobiography* or a life of him would have been a good introduction. No schoolboy could fail to respond to the life of Faraday. Even chemistry might have gained some adventitious interest through the life of Sir Humphry Davy; that would have combined the appeal of a brilliant success-story with that of Cornish patriotism.

Fairly soon the schoolboy is capable of a psychological intuition that adults are apt to forget and overlook. (One should not forget that Elizabethan schoolboys were capable of the emotional range of playing Shakespeare's heroines, and remembering that one may understand a lot.) Quite soon a critical interest in character develops and is ripened by observing the mutual exchanges of Mary Tudor and Elizabeth, or of Elizabeth and Mary Stuart, the part played in our history by such harridans as Margaret of Anjou and Henrietta Maria, or by such incompetent, if pious, fools as Henry VI and James II. Dr Keatinge quotes as an example of a document to study the remarkable letter Queen Elizabeth wrote to James of Scotland on the execution of his mother. It is an extraordinary psychological study; there is the whole complex situation written in brief in it: the sense of guilt, the Queen defending herself for what was an act of political necessity, a hateful dilemma imposed on her; in the same sentence asserting her innocence and yet that the step was justified; there is her anxiety at what James will do; a genuine regret mingled with relief that now it is all over: there is both sincerity and insincerity in it; ending up with propitiation and the hint of a bribe, the suggestion of common interest, that if James plays her game all will yet be well for him. *What* a document! *What* a woman! one feels as one reads it. And yet I think that almost any boy or girl would recognize the psychological subtlety of it and see the situation from the letter.

The truth is that there is no subject that more demands judgement or develops it more naturally. And it is judgement of human beings and their affairs, of motives and causes of action and its effects, that history develops; with natural science, not: it is a technical judgement that is there developed.

The adolescent schoolboy of today, growing up into the contemporary world with its ubiquitous cynicism and its cheap disbeliefs, becomes very much alive – as people in general in the Victorian age were not – to the gap between people's pretensions and their real motives, to the illusions they cherish, and –

still more extraordinary – the way they hold on to them even when they know they are illusions, to the half-conscious game of double bluff that people play with themselves and with others. A schoolboy, from the oldest of English schools, had something of this in his mind when he asked me quite recently whether the study of history did not make one completely sceptical. The answer is that it does make one salutarily sceptical of pretensions, and the larger and more high-sounding they are the more one has to beware – one is so used to that kind of thing in history, one has so often been there before. One develops a keen scent for humbug in all its forms: one knows that what people put forward as the universally good is almost always something that suits their own interest. It is probably the moralist that is the easiest prey to humbug; it is so very near to his usual stock-in-trade. The historian is hardly to be caught out this way; he has seen it at work too often in too many climes at too many times. Of course, he has his own dangers: he is apt to be bored by human silliness in so many different forms and guises, to throw up the sponge and say nothing can be done with human beings or for them, that they are unteachable and irredeemable (as they often seem to be), that the truth about human affairs is that *Tout passe, tout casse, tout lasse*. In short the historian's danger *is* scepticism, indifference; his temptation, despair.

Yet it is perhaps significant that though all historians have some scepticism, and some have been morally indifferent, not one has completely despaired – as some great writers have despaired. Not even Hume or Gibbon, or Voltaire, or for that matter Machiavelli. The answer to the intelligent schoolboy is that if there is much folly in the human record, there is also much greatness; if there is insincerity and hypocrisy and selfishness there is even more sincerity, single-mindedness, goodness of heart – and these are to be found everywhere, though never more notably than among the greatest and most gifted of men. As against man's cruelty one must fairly place his infinite capacity for self-sacrifice. One can go further and say that on the whole history shows – as life does, but history proves it – that it is better to be honest and true than to be bad, however clever

one may be. The Hitlers and William Rufuses and Richard IIIs
are apt to come to sticky ends. And though in human affairs
innocence is sometimes betrayed and goodness defeated, the
balance shown by history as on a chart – and nowhere else can
you see it – is indubitably the other way. It really does pay to
tell the truth and stick to it, to be courageous (without being
foolhardy), to work hard and do one's duty, to love well and
truly. That schoolboy's question brings us up against the difficult
intellectual issues treated in the last chapter; well aware of the
doubts they arouse and of their corrosive influence upon the
modern mind, I can reply simply that the effect of studying history is to make one a realist, possibly a little pessimistic – but
never a cynic. In short, in old-fashioned language, history is a
school of virtue.

These things apply with still more force at the university
stage of education, for it is then that the reasoning faculties
come more fully into play and young men develop the quality
of intellectual judgement. What is it that the study of history at
the university can do for one in this regard?

Perhaps I may refer to my own personal experience to bring
the point home. At school my attitude to history was emotional
and passionate; it was an affair of prejudices, of sympathies
and of repugnances. For example, my emotions were on the side
of King and Church in the civil war. I now recognize, though
my likes and dislikes remain the same, that it was the moderate
Parliamentarians who had most right with them, and that the
Parliamentary way was the right way through to the future. My
emotional preferences were hardly Protestant, certainly not Puritan; but I have no doubt now that the Protestant Reformation
was the making of England's fortune. So far from regretting it –
and there were regrettable sides to it, notably the destruction
of the monasteries and the dispersal of their treasures – yet we
cannot be grateful enough to the (sometimes unattractive)
Henricians and Edwardians who pushed us through it.

There are plenty of historians who allow their emotional prejudices to bedevil their judgement. Their reason is at the service
of their emotions; their emotions mould their reason. Take

Belloc and Chesterton as examples, those two big bouncing boys of prejudice, who had a deplorable influence in their day in rewriting our history and making nonsense of it. With them it is only too obvious. But it is no less obvious, to anyone who understands a little psychology, with a much subtler mind, Newman. If you read his novel *Loss and Gain* – which is very revealing of himself – you will see how all his sympathies at school were with King and Church. He never got over them. The whole of his subsequent mental history was a subtle process of finding intellectual reasons to justify what his heart had long ago opted for.

Le cœur a ses raisons, it has been said ; and it may be thought an uncomfortable state of affairs to have the reasons of the heart on one side and those of the mind on the other. But is one to prefer one's own comfort to intellectual honesty?

What has the study of history to offer to the mind's development at the university? What are the faculties that it elicits and strengthens? What are its effects? Naturally it does not cover the whole ground of a young man's mental development, any more than any other special discipline does, languages or one of the sciences or philosophy. Though in itself it covers only a part of the ground, it is wider, more general and diverse than any other subject. That gives a clue to the kind of mind that it appeals to and the quality of mind that it brings out. History is not a subject for a narrow, niggling, precise mind ; let him take to logic or economics. It needs a capacious and extensive, rather than intensive, kind of mind. It offers the advantage that attaches to Bacon's 'Reading maketh a full man'. He goes on to say that writing makes an 'exact' man. History sets a premium on accuracy, on adherence to fact. It is no use having a general impression that the battle of Waterloo took place somewhere or other, or at another time than it did. The thing that chiefly impresses me most about my colleagues who are historians is their natural accuracy of mind, accuracy to fact and circumstance. Lawyers have an even greater and more precise accuracy, a greater verbal exactness. For a combination of subtlety with precision one looks to the philosophers or logicians, or to the mathematicians – but they do not speak the language of common humanity.

History is also, as we have already seen, a science of judgement. It is all the time concerned with human beings and their affairs, public and private, social and individual; so that even at school it elicits judgement of human conduct, for it is an extension of our common-sense experience of it. (History is, then, a school of common sense.) At the university a further, more special development of judgement comes into play. History rests on documents of various kinds – landscape, buildings, monuments, books, papers, deeds, letters, inscriptions, scraps, sherds; and the teaching of history at the university is much concerned with the interpretation of documents. This introduces a point well put by Dr Keatinge: 'In history, as opposed to natural science, the fact which is at hand for observation is not the historical fact, but merely a description of it, and in many, if not in most cases, a very unreliable one. The transition from the document to the fact is difficult, occupies a great part of the historian's time, and dictates to him the nature of his method. In history there is thus an additional, and frequently a very uncertain step, which is not to be found to the same extent in natural science.' It is, therefore, that Seignobos tells us that 'all historical knowledge being indirect, history is essentially a science of reasoning'.

It is on account of the *general* character of the subject, its essential concern with human affairs, that Bacon is enabled to say that where the poets make man 'witty; the mathematics, subtle; natural philosophy, deep; moral, grave; logic and rhetoric, able to contend . . . histories make men wise'.

Though it does not compete with philosophy on its own ground, the study of history is not without some abstract value. As we have seen, it opens up intellectual problems of its own, problems that have more importance for us than many of the metaphysical problems that have consumed so much time and attention in the past. As an undergraduate studying history at Oxford my mind became increasingly possessed by the problems discussed in the last chapter, the issues of historical relativism and scepticism, the doctrines of, and questions raised by,

Marxism. Confronting these problems and struggling to think my way through them formed a major part of my intellectual development and helped me to work out my own position for myself. Perhaps I may contrast a contemporary at Oxford, the communist writer, Ralph Fox. He never ceased to regret to me that he had not read history, instead of languages. It meant for him that he had not an intellectual position of his own on these questions that have been so crucial for our generation. For want of it, he followed the 'Party line' : it sent him to a nameless grave in Spain, along with other good Englishmen superfluously sacrificed to an alien orthodoxy.

The study of history leads straight to an informed, and responsible, concern with politics. This book shows why : politics is the continuation of history in our time, it is history being made under our eyes. One is impelled therefore by the very nature of one's studies to take a closer interest in public affairs. If one's subject is the dissection of frogs, or the beauties of number, one's impulse towards politics is (I fancy) less strong. At the same time, the fact that one's study is history should give one a better basis for political judgement ; most people's political judgement is hopeless for want of such a basis. The increase of interest in politics among students at the universities between the wars went hand in hand with the development of the History Schools in them. At the beginning of this century Professor A. F. Pollard could lament that modern history was the Cinderella of London University, and certainly he cites an incredibly small number of students. Gone are those days ; he himself changed all that at London University, which now has one of the largest history faculties in Britain. At Oxford the School of Modern History is the largest of all the Schools, and in addition there are the ancient historians who form part of the Greats faculty. The Oxford School may be regarded as the leading one in Britain, not only on account of size, but because it exports its products to staff the history departments of so many other universities. The famous Manchester School was an offshoot of Oxford, its leading figures – Tout and Tait, Powicke, Namier, Galbraith, E. F. Jacob – all Oxford men. So too at Birmingham with Sir Richard Lodge, or at Edinburgh with Basil

Williams, B. H. Sumer and Richard Pares. Nor is the export of Oxford-trained historians confined to Britain: they are to be found in all the universities of the Commonwealth, and in many of the United States. The Cambridge School, though smaller, is of particular distinction, and in recent years has been more productive, proportionately, in historical research and writing. Many admirable works of scholarship have been coming from Cambridge. At Oxford historians tend to sacrifice their own work to their teaching – though to this it owes its seminal influence.

It is interesting to note how many of the younger generation of politicians in the House of Commons elected in 1945, with a Labour majority, graduated from History and Modern Greats, and politically through the University Labour Club, at Oxford. During the last twenty years in my experience the association has been very close; and I have shown that there is a reason for it. Two generations ago they would have come from the Greats School – classics and ancient history – as Asquith and Grey did, Morley and Bryce, Curzon and Lang, and many others, like Sir Robert Morant, whose names are not so well known but who have left their mark in our history.

It is remarkable too how many of the contemporary generation of writers have come from the History School at Oxford: Guedalla, Arthur Bryant, Michael Sadleir, Aldous Huxley; Cyril Connolly, Evelyn Waugh, Graham Greene; Lord David Cecil, C. V. Wedgwood. It is a matter of melancholy pride that the two most gifted poets of the last war, Alun Lewis and Sidney Keyes, were both historians, where their predecessors of the last war, Rupert Brooke and Wilfred Owen, were classicists and linguists.

A word about the organization of the School that occupies such a central place in university education may be useful. It is dominated by the Final Examination to which reading and teaching are directed over a course of three years. There are three papers that cover the whole of English history, dividing it up into three periods. In my time there were separate papers on political, constitutional and economic history. I regard it as an improvement that those divisions were abolished – an improvement with which the argument of this book is in line. For it is much less valuable to read political history divorced from constitutional, and constitutional divorced from economic history. It is more stimulating and suggestive to see how these things act and react upon one another; it is more fertilizing to the life of the mind to grasp them in association with each other, and in any case closer to the truth of things and the way they happen. The most fascinating questions, regarded academically, are often borderline questions: they tended to be left out formerly; not so now. There is a fourth paper on the constitutional documents of English history, either medieval or modern with passages from set books and statutes. Altogether the background is mainly English history, the core of the School. Plenty of scope for the widest capacity and reflection – one can never cover it all equally or read enough to please oneself, let alone the examiners. The documents are a test of accuracy, attention to detail, ability to interpret – besides the light they throw on the history.

Next, there are two papers on a selected period of foreign history, usually covering something like a century. One may choose almost any period one likes; the most popular is the more recent from the French revolution on to today. And that is quite right on Bury's principle that modern history is more important to study. At the same time one does not want everybody studying the same period; and it is a good thing that the next most popular stretch is the sixteenth century, that of Renaissance and Reformation out of which modern Europe (except Russia and the Balkans) emerges. Then there is a special subject, which must be taken by those who aspire to a good class: a wide range of historical subjects from which to choose, from St Augustine to modern Labour movements. Two papers are set, one of which is given up to the documents and original authorities for the subject. The purpose of this is obvious: a more searching test of accuracy, attention to detail, and of the interpretation and use of evidence.

There are two general papers, more abstract in character. One in political theory, which is based on the study of Aristotle's *Politics*, Hobbes's *Leviathan* and Rousseau's *Contrat Social* as texts and on the history of modern political theory; the other dealing with general questions of historical method and research, the intellectual issues that arise in connection with history, aspects of the history of culture, of art and historical literature. This is a new paper since my time as an undergraduate, and one that goes to fill a need which I felt strongly as a young tutor. There was far too little opportunity for this kind of general discussion of the issues raised by the subject, especially as compared with Greats for example; one reason for the superiority of Greats over Modern History as a School. It will be seen that the weakness of the History School, as compared with Greats (ancient history and philosophy) and Modern Greats (philosophy, politics and economics), is on the abstract side. Things have the defects of their qualities. These two papers do something to rectify the balance, which necessarily in history is on the side of the factual and concrete. Lastly there is a paper of translation from foreign languages; the student of modern history is expected to know two, Latin and one modern language.

Such is the structure of the Final Honours School of Modern History to which reading and teaching are directed at Oxford. It determines the plan of a student's work during his three years' course – he reads towards the end of that examination; though in the life of a residential university there is time for a good deal of reading outside his work. It is even more important, and more to the real purpose of a university, that he should become a cultivated man than that he should get a good class in the Schools. I recommend both.

It is not my purpose to describe the whole organization of historical study at Oxford – professors, readers, lecturers, tutors; libraries, societies, clubs; writing and research. That would demand a book in itself. My object has simply been to provide an illustration of the use of history in educating the young student at a university and how it works.

I have gone in somewhat undue detail into the shape of historical study and the School at Oxford, but it may be taken as fairly representative, with changes of emphasis here and there, of British universities as a whole.

Now for a word of criticism. It is obvious that at a time when the United States has become the dominant power in the Western world, nothing like enough attention is paid in Britain to American history, political institutions and thought. This is the more surprising and unimaginative in that the United States, after all, is the greatest thing, along with the Commonwealth, that the English-speaking peoples have achieved.

It is true that the study of American history is increasing at British universities, and that valuable contributions to the subject are being made by British scholars in this field. But American history and literature should enter in a more significant way into general education, particularly at universities. Especially since those subjects are becoming ever more relevant to our own society, civilization and fate ; especially since the separate histories of our peoples are tending to merge into one wide stream, and we are becoming, in Churchill's famous phrase, 'somewhat mixed up together'.

In any case, the British outlook in these matters of history, literature and civilization is somewhat too insular and nationally confined, insufficiently flexible and open to outer currents and experience. The result of two shattering wars has been to make British historians less in touch with Continental thought and scholarship than before 1914. Britain is more in touch with, and dependent upon, America than ever before ; but this is not properly expressed, or significantly grounded, in university courses and studies as yet.

Meanwhile, the United States has become increasingly self-conscious of, and absorbed in, her own history, mission, character, culture, destiny – too much so, though remaining more open and sympathetic to world-civilization and the oecumenical approach than Britain, more engaged and concerned. All the same, the older American interest in the origins of their history, politics, culture, in Britain – which led to so many masterly works from scholars in those fields – has relatively declined, with America's absorbed interest in herself. And this is a pity, for the origins remain what they were, as important as before.

One expression of this is the far less attention paid to the colonial period in American history, compared with the disproportionate concentration on the periods of the revolution and civil war, particularly the latter, which has of late reached rather absurd proportions.

On the other hand American universities pay more attention to courses in the history of civilization, where the British might well follow.

History and Culture:
Further Uses and Pleasures

History is an essential part of the mind of a cultivated
man. One may be a cultivated man without knowing mathematics or chemistry or engineering, for those are specialisms.
We expect the technicians in question to know them and to do
our sums and sanitation for us. But some knowledge of history,
or even more a sense of history, is a necessary part of the
self-awareness of our environment. In nothing is the degree of
cultivation of a man more clearly revealed.

An uneducated man has no sense of history. He does not
know whether the house he sees is Victorian or Georgian, Elizabethan or medieval ; or what that means if told. He cannot tell
whether it is beautiful or not ; he has no means of judging, no
sense of standards -- for that, as Plato would say, is part of the
same subject. Travelling up to the North Country the other day
with a friend who is an historian, we were commenting on the
buildings that caught our attention as we passed through
strange towns. A friendly soldier in the same compartment was
astonished that we could tell at a glance roughly the dates when
many of them were built. Yet there is nothing remote or difficult about that; anyone would have thought that we had
achieved the differential calculus ; whereas in fact it is open
to anybody to get the hang of the building styles of different
periods quite easily. And think of the interest it adds to knock-
ing about the country ! Most people go about the country with
their eyes closed. It is from their ignorance and insensibility
that the progressive ruin of the countryside, the wrecking of
our old towns – they had the most beautiful urban architecture
in the world – the hideousness of much of the new arises.

How well I remember from earlier days car-rides about the

country with the uneducated: nothing more exquisitely agoniz-
ing; no perception of the difference between this and that, between this that was beautiful – in fact, that they didn't like – and
something else that was appalling; people who thought the
place 'finely improved' when it had been thoroughly disfigured
by a row of mean bungalows on the Cornish cliffs. The vast
majority of people belong to that category. But that does not
mean that there are no standards, or that there is any doubt
about them. The standards are quite well known to those who
know; those who don't, do not know them; standards are set
by those who know, as they always have been. They are historically based; they spring out of long tradition, though the
test of their value is an aesthetic one.

What is the purpose in my saying this? What good aim may
be served by it? *To help as many people as possible to share in
the mental life of civilized, cultivated people.* The world is as-
tray not because people are wicked or irremediably stained
with some original sin, but for lack of cultivation, intelligence,
reason, sense. I am going to be quite blunt and say what educated people really think about the uneducated. Hardly anybody ever dares to; there is a conspiracy not to, though we hear
more than enough in contemporary literature of what uneducated people think of the educated. The loss is on the side of the
uneducated; it is really not fair to them. I propose to reverse
matters and to tell them.

There is nothing more boring for educated people in the
society of the uneducated than the restriction of their conversation, the limitation of their mental world. Their horizon is
restricted to the parish, in the country; in the towns, to the
radius of the local cinemas or T.V.; their sense of what is going
on is crude and irrational; they have no means of judging or
appraising events, of which, in consequence, they are victims.
And there is nothing to talk to them about – except perhaps
sex. (I know, for I have attempted the difficult experiment of
continuing to live in touch with an original social environment
on a lower level than my interests of mind; most people, on
growing out if it, have done with it. There are some advantages
to be gained from the point of view of social observation, to

set against the acute discomforts, mainly of an aesthetic character.)

No good purpose is served by our being defeatist. Far too many intelligent people are too diffident and give the case away to the Philistines and barbarians. Quite unnecessarily and unfairly; it is perhaps most of all unfair to the low-brows, who never arrive at the point of knowing what it is that keeps these others so interested and lively and releases them from being the preys of boredom.

The simple truth is that it is inexhaustibly interesting to have an active mental life. For one thing, one is much less at the mercy of external circumstances. There is no end to the voyaging and explorations one can do. During the war it was impossible for a great many people to travel, in space; but it was all the more delightful to voyage in time, and, for that matter, in space too. It is that that accounts for the marked growth of historical reading during the war and the long winters of blackout. A businessman of my acquaintance told me that for the first time he had taken up reading, mainly history, during the war, and of the extraordinary difference it had made to his enjoyment of life: the opening out of new horizons of illimitable interest, the widening of perspective in which to view what happens around us – altogether something approaching in its effect to a conversion.

I recall from experience in Cornwall what interest uneducated people get from the lectures, excursions and readings of Old Cornwall Societies. In fact they get the beginnings of education from them: they learn to *see* things, old places and buildings, churches and holy-wells, castles and camps, stone-circles and crosses, the evidence and survivals of times past. They begin to get a grasp of what the life of communities has been, of which they are a part; they develop a sense of its continuity; they become proud of their heritage. Who can deny that this is a good thing, however unfinished and crude it may be? And how infinitely better than the appalling vacuity, without savour or sense, coarse and adrift, deriving the character of its ideas from T.V. or comic strips, its standards of behaviour from bar and street-corner, of the bulk of the illiterate. The great

majority of people see nothing, hear nothing, know nothing, and
– it is hardly surprising – in consequence understand nothing,
appreciate nothing, or nothing very much.

It is all very well to turn your back on the things of the mind
when you are young and active and can run and ride and swim
and make love. I am all in favour of enjoyment: that is part of
my gospel. But the things of the mind and of the spirit are to
be enjoyed too. Let us have no inhibitions on either side. It is
bad to inhibit the life of the body; it is equally bad to inhibit
the life of the mind. The low-brows are just as wrong as the
kill-joys. What one needs is to strike a balance, to achieve a
due harmony so that the one can refresh and enliven the other.

It follows that in the days of youth and health and strength
you need to take some interest in the things of the mind, even
if you are not naturally inclined to; for as you get older and
physical resources fail you, you need something to fall back on.
Actually one's interest in the things of the mind, once it has got
root or is released, deepens and becomes riper as one grows
older. And so with history. Our appreciation and understanding
of it, our feeling for its subtleties and excitements grows with
us as we get older, instead of failing us. As we grow less good at
mounting the hills we get better at seeing the place of Christianity in the development of our civilization, at understanding
what we owe to it and what it did for us, in civilizing the barbarian peoples; at appreciating the incomparable miracle that
was Greece; at seeing Italy and France, from which we have
derived so much, with discernment; at watching with loving
interest the unfolding of the picture of life.

There is something childish about the uncultivated man. Not
to have a sense of time is like having no ear or sense of beauty
– it is to be bereft of a faculty. It reminds me of a child I heard
the other day, standing before a case of exhibits of the Elizabethan age in the Victoria and Albert Museum and asking:
'Were you born then, Mummy?' But she was about seven or
eight. The time-sense of most uneducated people is equally
childish: they are not adult.

Even educated people lose a lot of the subtlety in understanding things through not looking at them historically. I never

cease to be taken aback by people's short-term judgements of nations and peoples – of the English, for example – on the basis of what they look like now. You cannot tell what a people really are until you see them in a long-term perspective. It is like expecting to know a man from one moment's look at him. And nations are much more complex.

No wonder people abroad were surprised by Britain's resistance in 1940. They need not have been, if only they had read our history. It was in our whole history and tradition to resist; we always had resisted in similar disasters and come through. Or consider the United States and the stupid conviction of the Germans that the Americans – because they were devoted to peace – were no fighters. Anyone knowing anything of American history knows that the civil war was one of the toughest and hardest-fought wars in history, and look at the long and irreconcilable resistance they put up in the War of Independence. We had learnt from that; nobody made any mistakes about it in Britain, in either of the two world wars.

People who do not know their history are liable to be fooled. I do not know whether to call not being fooled a use or a pleasure – it has the elements of both. But indeed we can now see that the dictators, Hitler and Mussolini and the Japanese warlords, were really too ignorant. There is nothing more dangerous than to be ignorant.

M. Maillaud in an interesting book *The English Way* tells us what the Continental view of the English is. 'The picture conjured up by the fairly well-educated Continental world presents the English as sporting, practical, sparing of words, businesslike, conservative, disciplined, either puritanical or oddly eccentric and melancholy.' That is a picture based on one reading of the Victorian age – even so, thoroughly inadequate. Nobody can think of the Victorian Englishman as 'sparing of words', the age of Dickens, Carlyle, Gladstone, Spurgeon, General Booth – all those orators on platforms or in pulpit. Nor was the earlier Englishman of the Elizabethan age, or the eighteenth century, either, 'sparing of words' or 'puritanical', 'disciplined' or 'melancholy'. There was always a genial, jovial quality about English social life, and Continentals of earlier centuries thought of us as the most indisciplined of peoples.* It was a mistake on the part of the dictators to think that the mood of appeasement betokened the decadence of the English people; underneath there were the old long-tried qualities patient and strong; held in restraint, but still there under the surface, was the spirit that had refused to yield to so many tyrants, and seen them out. It would be a similar mistake to underestimate the toughness and fighting qualities of the Americans because they are essentially a civilian people.

It is most important for a nation to have a rational and true tradition of its own history: one that makes sense of the past and makes events and their upshot intelligible. It is an essential factor in the strength and coherence of a people, a chief element in their success and effectiveness. In the end, a false historical tradition is a terrible source of weakness and intellectual disarray, even though in the short run it promises to give a people greater cohesion, and pride in their past, and hence operate as a stimulus to action. Nations can be over-stimulated to disaster by short-term readings of their past. Neither Hitler nor Mussolini had any real sense of history, though each was cheaply and egotistically excited by melodramatic readings of history. The dream of modern Italy as an imperial power, the Mediterranean as ‘mare nostrum’ and the rest of it, was indeed a nostrum that cost Italy thousands of lives, and ended in nothing but wreckage, impoverishment and humiliation.

The influence upon Germans of a false reading of history has been even more tragic, for Germans have a strong tendency to believe only that which they wish to think. Even now after the nightmare experience they brought upon themselves and the world, by their pursuit of the dream of world-power as the logical end of the process of German history, they have still not learnt the essential lesson. Karl Barth tells us that ‘the real discussion has not started so long as one talks to the Germans only about Hitler. The crucial point is reached when the discussion comes to Bismarck. When the Nazi plaster has fallen away in dust there is revealed in the majority of Germans, even in those

---

* cf. my The English Spirit, pp. 23–4.

who have been active in opposition, the solid brickwork of German nationalism. They regard Nazism as a regrettable incident, but all before it is beyond criticism. They do not understand that Nazism was nothing else than the final outcome of the Bismarckian policy, which forged Germany with blood and iron into a National Socialist, capitalist, imperialist Reich, and so into the grave-digger of the vital freedom of 1848.'

Nothing could be more important for them than that they should understand the real significance of the career of Bismarck (or, for that matter, of Luther) : how Bismarck's determination to eliminate liberalism, constitutional government, any form of democracy, stunted and eventually withered the development of responsible self-government in the German people ; how his unification of Germany by force, the concentration upon military power, reduced European politics to those terms, and eventually produced a reply to the challenge that power was to the security of everybody else. It was Bismarck more than anybody who set Germany's feet upon the wrong path ; and yet Germans for the most part have no conception of it.

The English have been willing to learn from the mistakes they made in the past. They have learned that there is no government like self-government. They made mistakes in relation to Ireland in the past – not that the fault was all one one side, or that all the mistakes were avoidable : some of them were in the nature of things. But in our time they learned to leave Ireland alone to work out her own salvation in her own way. The moral was next drawn in regard to India. A conscious attempt was made in imperial policy in the nineteenth century to avoid the mistakes made in the treatment of the American Colonies : hence the unexpected success, on the whole, of the record with regard to Canada and the generous return the Canadians made in this century of Britain's peril.

Above all, we learned from the disruption of government and society in the civil war of the seventeenth century, or rather, our governing class learned, and handed down what they had learnt to become the operative tradition of our policy, shared in progressively by all. After the fires of fanaticism had burned down and men had learned from sad experience the futility of it – in Samuel Butler's famous summing up of it all in *Hudibras*, 'When men fell out they knew not why' – sensible people led the country towards toleration, common sense and moderation. A significant expression of this spirit was the founding of the Royal Society at the Restoration in 1660. Of even wider consequence for society was the Whig revolution of 1688, without bloodshed, a triumph for the middle way. It formalized and made permanent in English institutions Parliamentarian and civic liberties, a measure of religious toleration, while retaining the useful initiative of the monarchy in government and its residual powers. This left the way clear, and made the processes easier, for further constitutional development.

As G. M. Trevelyan says in his admirable summing up of the matter in his book, *The Revolution of 1688*, the men who made it may not have been very nice or noble spirits, but they were very clever men, wise and sensible. The settlement they then made lasted, and provided a satisfactory foundation upon which Britain proceeded to make the commercial, maritime and colonial achievements of the eighteenth century, and to build the first British Empire.

At its overthrow and dissolution with the American revolution, the leaders of the latter were again much inspired by the tradition of 1688, and followed a similar moderate, conservative course in creating the institutions and modelling the political character of the new United States.

Professor Butterfield tells us in *The Englishman and his History* that the Whig interpretation of our past has been a formative element in this process. 'The common law and the Whig interpretation have worked together to tighten the bonds that hold the Englishman to his past – have helped to foster our love of precedent, our affection for tradition, our desire for gradualness in change, our adherence to ancient liberties.' In our own time we have seen this Whig view, with its emphasis on individual liberty, moderation and common sense, absorb what might have been a Tory alternative, the epic story of British expansion overseas. 'Perhaps only in the shock of 1940,' he says, 'did we realize to what a degree the British Empire had become an organization for the purpose of liberty. What power is in this English tradition which swallows up monarchy, Toryism, imperialism, yet leaves each of them still existing, each part of a wider synthesis.' I would only add that the grandest part of that epic story of the expansion of our stock is concerned with America ; the United States is not outside the tradition ; it is its greatest vindication – of the Whigs in particular.

Professor Butterfield goes on to analyse what is at the core of this political sense. He says that a recognizable element is 'the feeling that, apart from any action we may take in some present conjuncture, the world is changing : and history is moving forward on her own account, and we ourselves must reckon with this process and use it – must conceive of ourselves as co operating with history, leaning on events somewhat ; not resting idle indeed, but lying in wait for opportunity.' He concludes that 'amongst all political crimes the attempt to fly in the face of history is the one that has suffered the heaviest retribution in the modern world'. He contrasts 'that tempered faith in the course of history' which is at the heart of the English tradition with the revolutionary course of some Continental countries : 'It is not clear that Continental countries, which have had their revolutions, followed by counter-revolutions, have greatly improved on the English rate of progress, in spite of what they paid in havoc and bloodshed precisely for the sake of speed.'

In France the revolution created a barrier, and still one is either on one side or on the other. It has impeded a unified conception of the past for the French, one making the history of France as a whole consistent and intelligible, doing justice to the work of both sides of that great divide.* As it is, French history is written too much in partisan terms, through either royalist monocles or republican pince-nez. The interesting minds are those that escape these limitations. As an example of royalist myopia carried to ridiculous lengths, we may take the case

---

*An exception to this, which does justice to both sides and makes French history as a whole intelligible, is Lucien Romier's *History of France*.

of the history text-book on which the little Comte de Chambord, the legitimist heir to the throne, was brought up : which described the creative, the epic period from 1789 to 1815 in the words, 'During these years the country was a prey to internal disruption.' It is not surprising that that boy grew up into the political ass who muffed his chances of the throne in the 1870s.

With this we reach the borderland between public use and private pleasures. Let us turn to the pleasures of conversation.

Since history is an extension, and a verification, of our experience it makes what is in itself a realm of delightful discourse one of intrinsic value. As a subject of conversation, compared with the weather, or bridge, or the dogs, it offers more variety, interest and scope for discussion. It offers too all the possibilities of what is the chief subject of conversation among Englishmen – politics.

It is one of the pleasures of life, lasting and satisfying, if sober and sedate, to enjoy the conversation of friends who are historians. One such is a medievalist, an authority on the fifteenth century, the period immediately preceding my special sphere of interest. We are in the habit of walking about the Oxfordshire countryside to see villages, houses, churches with their tombs and monuments ; farms, pastures, wolds. The countryside comes alive for us in conversation, is peopled once more by the folk who lived their lives in these places and made a figure here centuries ago. As often as not they turn up in the churches, at Stanton Harcourt or Minster Lovell, Swinbrook or Asthall or Burford ; at Bibury, Ablington, Winson or Colne Rogers ; at Compton Beauchamp, Ashbury, Ashdown or Uffington ; at Cricklade or Lechlade, Ampney Crucis or Fairford ; Wallingford or Bensington or Ewelme, where Chaucer's granddaughter, the Duchess, lies in state.

While we walk we talk ; no lack of things to talk about ; nothing of that boredom which is the torment of the uncultivated. (As Dean Inge said, 'the true intellectual is never bored'.) Another historian friend with whom I walk knows about the seventeenth century. What more natural than to ask him questions about the people whom I know about in the sixteenth century and what happened to them and their families? Other friends of mine provide me with information about the eighteenth century or are open to being questioned about the issues of policy in debate then and that have affected us in so many ways since. Or there are the delightful lunch-hour walks and talks with fellow-historians at the Huntington Library in California, from which I profit so much, particularly in the field of American history.

These pleasures of conversation offer more than the pleasures of gossip. There is poetry in them; behind it all, that sense of the underside of life, its continuity and its pathos: all that hardly expressed, though it is there all the time like the sounds and scents of the countryside we are passing through, the music of a stream by the wayside (as it might be Eamont or Fal or Windrush), the steady noise of the wind in the trees like the sound of the sea, or dappled light and shadow brushing the blue bells of campanulas that spread over the banks of Grimsdyke. There is all the latent appeal to the imagination, hardly talked of, yet understood between us. A student away at the war wrote me: 'I acknowledge, gladly and proudly, that you and I share very fully the pleasures of appreciating music and literature; our countryside, too, architecture and art. But I wonder if you know how sour for me are the grapes of history, whose study, based as it is on years of intellectual effort more intense than I am capable of, yields you more solid joys, more lasting *pleasure*.' Anyone who starts with a defeatist view like that weakens himself from the beginning, and this student in the event failed to make much of his chances. It is bad psychology to start off a defeatist: one never knows what one can do until one tries.

On a more prosaic level, there is so much to discuss, the fascinating patterns of motive, the intricacies of character, the astonishing stories that some people's lives make, the detective-thriller interest in tracking them down and where they lived, the ghosts.

A great deal of history may be learned, in the most congenial way, by reading biographies. We all know what Carlyle thought: 'Social life is the aggregate of all the individual men's lives who constitute society; history is the essence of innumerable biographies.' And again, on the lives of great men: 'As I

take it, universal history, the history of what man has accomplished in this world, is at bottom the history of the great men
who have worked here. They were the leaders of men, these
great ones: the modellers, patterns, and in a wide sense crea-
tors, of whatsoever the general mass of men contrived to do or
to attain; all things that we see standing accomplished in the
world are properly the outer material result, the practical real-
ization and embodiment, of thoughts that dwelt in the great
men sent into the world.' Without going all the way with Carlyle in this, we can agree with the more limited proposition he
goes on to. 'One comfort is that great men, taken up in any
way, are profitable company. We cannot look, however
imperfectly, upon a great man, without gaining something by
him.'

That is enough for our purpose; it follows that reading biographies is of value in itself. A first-rate biography will lead you
straight into the atmosphere, the thoughts, will give you the
very pulse, of the period. Many classical scholars would agree
that Plutarch's *Lives* forms the best introduction to Ancient
Greece and Rome. Or take the greatest of English biographies,
Boswell's *Life of Johnson*. It is a wonderful picture of an age
and a society, that remarkable society of which Dr Johnson was
the centre and easily the dominating figure. You hear them
talking, you overhear what they thought about each other;
more subtly, you can sense the atmosphere, the standards and
values, the conventions and prejudices, of the time. Then there
are the characters, more varied, more convincing than any
novel, and of far more remarkable people: there is equable Sir
Joshua; shy, touchy Goldsmith, constant target for the Doctor's sallies; irresistible David Garrick, vain as any actor must
be, whose relations with Johnson, though intimate, were difficult, for the younger Garrick had early found the success that
came so late and with so much reluctance to Johnson; the
conceited, affected Gibbon with his precise manner, who said
nothing in that company but took in everything. And then the
Doctor himself; how to describe him? Impossible; one can but
go to Boswell.

Or what a portrait of the Victorian age we have through a

leading figure, a central one in intellectual society, in Proude's *Life of Carlyle*. Good critics think this is the first of our modern biographies: it certainly marked a change from the conventional Victorian biography in the critical candour of its treatment of the subject. All the more admirable considering Froude's veneration of Carlyle. There was an outcry at Froude's failure to treat the subject with the usual humbug, and on the book's appearance one well-known lady destroyed all the letters she had received from famous men. The *Life of Carlyle* took ten years of Froude's life and as many more of controversy. But Froude was too good an historian not to know that the finest respect to Carlyle was to paint him – warts and all; and in fact there emerged a speaking portrait of a man of genius, with his gifts and qualities and defects. Froude thought it his best book. Apart from much else, it is a large slice of the intellectual history of the nineteenth century.

A lesser masterpiece, cheerful and congenial, is Sir G. O. Trevelyan's *Life and Letters of Macaulay*. That depicts a different, though no less remarkable, circle and one that was even more representative of the Victorian age and its characteristic beliefs and outlook. Or for an earlier period and for a man of genius greater than either of them, read Lockhart's *Life of Sir Walter Scott* – second only to Boswell's *Johnson* among English biographies. These and others like them make delightful reading, easy of approach, sympathetic in their primary interest in personality, in the story of a human being; they are informative of the society to which their subjects belonged and they add up to a portrait of the past which is a living possession of the present. For the past is not over and done with, but *lives* in such books.

The biographies of men of action provide the most useful introductions to the periods their lives so much affected. I do not propose to enter here into the exact character of the influence of great men in history, even if it could be defined; but no one can deny that, within limits, the action of such a person at a critical stage may be decisive. It is interesting to watch the difficulties that a would-be orthodox Marxist like Trotsky has in allowing for the decisive influence of Lenin in the Russian revolution; it is the most curious part of his history of the revolution. Yet however much the revolution owed to Lenin, nothing would have come of him and his movement if he had not been presented with his chance in 1917. The point is that he was prepared for it and knew how to use it.

It is often, therefore, a useful way of summing up a significant theme in history to view it through the career of the man indissolubly connected with it: to see the end of the Roman republic and the beginnings of the Empire through the life of Julius Caesar, the Puritan revolution and the civil war in this country through that of Cromwell, the culmination of the French revolution and its spirit of militant aggression in the career of Napoleon. Naturally, the biography of even the most dominating of historical figures does not exhaust the interest of the theme and period; one needs to see the end of the Roman republic through the career of Cicero as well as Caesar, the French revolutionary period through Robespierre as well as Napoleon.

I have already mentioned (Chapter 2) the use and pleasure there are in reading history in enriching our appreciation of literature. Here I should emphasize how much of historical writing is itself good literature. When young we are apt to think that literature means poetry and plays, novels, short stories, essays. As we grow older we realize that history is just as much literature and that the great historians are great writers as much as the poets and novelists. Perhaps history requires a more mature appreciation and corresponds to a ripening of taste. Many people who liked reading novels or poetry when young come to prefer reading biography and memoirs, or letters and diaries, later on. It is easier to appreciate the *Vicar of Wakefield* than the *Decline and Fall of the Roman Empire*; but there is no doubt which is the greater work. Clarendon is one of the best writers of the later seventeenth century. Hume's *History* is not unworthy of the philosopher, and brought him more success and fame in his own day than his philosophical writings. Or what are we to say of the rich array of historians in the nineteenth century? Carlyle, Macaulay, Froude – they are not inferior to the novelists of that fertile, creative age.

Nor must we forget how many of the writers whose main achievements were elsewhere have been attracted by history and made their contributions to it. Sir Thomas More wrote his life of Edward V, as Bacon his history of Henry VII. We all know how much of English history may be learned from Shakespeare's plays. Hobbes wrote his history of the civil war, Milton his *History of Britain*. Newman wrote a good deal on the subject, Kingsley less, though his enthusiasm for the Elizabethan age – caught from his brother-in-law, Froude – is the making of *Westward Ho!* Even Dickens, least historically-minded of writers, wrote his *Child's History of England*; Thackeray, steeped in the eighteenth century, made a direct contribution with his *Four Georges*, and a more valuable indirect one with *Henry Esmond*. When we come to Kipling and Hardy, we find each in his way impregnated with the sense of history. Kipling, like Dickens, attempted a text-book history of England, though his real perception of it was imaginative and is to be found in *Puck of Pook's Hill* and *Rewards and Fairies*. Though Hardy lived through the great war of 1914–18, his mind was possessed, as T. E. Lawrence found when he visited him, by the Napoleonic war: *that* was the great war to him, upon which his imagination brooded, to produce such masterpieces as *The Trumpet Major* and *The Dynasts*.

A knowledge of history enriches even our appreciation of music, most rarefied of the arts and the most *sui generis*. Perhaps we may return to the passage quoted on page 111 where Trevelyan says: 'Music needs no such historic introduction to be fully appreciated, for it is not allusive, or only slightly.' But not quite so. It is true that the appreciation of music is of its own kind, a musical experience. Over and above that, it is full of allusions, and there is always the allusion to its own time and period, of which it is the most intimate revelation possible. When you listen to Bach and hear the dance-rhythms of gigue and courante, sarabande or bourrée or polonaise, it is as if you can see those figures of the eighteenth century weaving their way in and out the patterns of the dance, slow and stately, or sprightly and gay, with their low bows and curtsies, the gentleman handing the ladies, the turns and rhythms so expressive of the equipoise, the deliberation of the age. There is a more staccato vigour, something more primitive in the jigs of the Elizabethans, a more solemn formality in their pavans. The melodies of Schubert have a direct relation to the popular music of the Vienna of his time ; it had even its response, if less direct, in the deep and philosophical spirit of Beethoven. Or how fully to appreciate the music of Palestrina without hearing it, as we would see a picture by Tintoretto, springing out of its proper time and circumstance : the sixteenth century, the polyphonic tradition, the religious conflict, the Renaissance impulse passing over into the Counter-Reformation, the renewal of faith? When you realize what the submergence of the Catholic faith and its persecution under Elizabeth meant to spirits like William Byrd, the pathos and tenderness of his settings of the Mass gain a new poignancy, the asseveration of his faith a deeper meaning in the motets he wrote for the feast of Corpus Christi.

With the music of our own time the thing becomes more complex, as with so much contemporary art ; it often has a direct reference to the art of a previous period, sometimes springs out of its very idiom. Just as Rex Whistler's painting refers back to the Regency, or Martyn Skinner's Letters to Malaya to the manner of the eighteenth century, so in a still deeper way with the music of Ravel and Vaughan Williams. With Ravel, as with Prokoviev, one sometimes gets the impression of the work being pastiche, he had such a acute sense of period and style, and such cleverness in reproducing them ; in Pavane pour une Infante Défunte it is the early seventeenth century, in the Tombeau de Couperin it is the mid seventeenth, in La Valse there is a Strauss waltz of the high nineteenth century, tricked out with all the resources of the twentieth in harmony and orchestration. All the same, this was the way in which Ravel thought ; the sense of a previous period released something in him, and stimulated him to create. So too with Vaughan Williams ; the music of the sixteenth century, of Tallis and Byrd, is his natural language, indeed he shares their experience ; he did not come to express himself fully until he had found himself in them. With him, more than with any other composer, the language of a previous age loosened his own tongue, released a creative impulse: a nostalgic spirit, replete with the sense of history.

The experience of music is perhaps the most inward way that is left to us of experiencing an age that is gone by. In it we can still hear its pulse, listen to its heart-beats still; in nothing are we more closely in touch with its very spirit, responding too, centuries afterwards, to the passions and regrets, the joys and griefs that moved those others in their day. In music they live for us still, out of time, the timeless.

*

With music I have taken the case of an art in which the historical element is at its least direct and least essential. At the other end of the scale is architecture, the most historical of the arts, where history is at its most obvious; one might even regard architecture as history arrested in stone, the movement of time congealed into plastic form. For at every point a building expresses the needs, the character, of its age. An old and complex building will bear the signs upon it of various ages which it has lived through. I think of a manor-house near Oxford which has a fragment of its medieval core; at the back it has an Elizabethan or Jacobean gable and a little seventeenth-century court; the front is plain, sober Georgian, but at one end a Regency bow-window is thrown out and at the other a Victorian conservatory. What generations of family-life, with their different circumstances and different ideas of domestic life, that agreeable *mélange* testifies to!

With a town there is infinitely greater variety. In almost any English town of any antiquity one moves easily from the Middle Ages in the parish church, elevated high above the houses around it, to the present day with its contrast between the public buildings put up by government departments – post-offices or employment exchanges – with their good standards of design, traditional or modern, and the appalling confusion of modern commercial buildings: the multiple concerns, the shops and petrol-filling stations, the meanness of the houses – all without tradition or dignity, without conscience or neighbourliness, vulgar, garish, uncivilized. How much of contemporary life that reflects! On the way between one and the other you may easily pick out fragments of the sixteenth or seventeenth centuries, possibly a Georgian terrace or street, Regency shopfronts or decent Victorian dwellings. Or think how well a Wren city church reflects that decorous and substantial society; family-religion, the spacious pew, the seats behind for the servants, the high pulpit, the sermon a chief feature of the service, morally edifying, common sense, prosy; one almost sees it all, Pepys ogling a pretty woman in the intervals of singing lustily from his book, lending a critical ear to the sermon, his attention wandering back to the lady across the way or thinking regretfully of Prue at home.

Or consider Oxford with its accent on the Middle Ages and the seventeenth century. One can see the society of the time reflected in the development of the college, parallel with that of the manor-house; the rather haphazard arrangement of the earliest medieval buildings at Merton, followed in the next century by the new model of a regular quadrangle, with an attached cloister, at New College. A century later, and the cloister is placed conveniently inside the quadrangle as at Magdalen for sheltered communication. Or one can watch the evolution of the T-shaped plan of the college chapel: or of the medieval domestic house with its hall and chambers through the Tudor and Stuart periods to the Georgian examples which have never been surpassed.

I have said little on the subject precisely because there is so much to be said about it: many books have been written on the history of architecture and on the relations of the two. History is the front-door approach to architecture, and almost every historian who is any good is keenly interested in it. The interest in these things and the pleasure they give are inexhaustible. For the reader's guidance I would suggest a little Victorian book that is still useful, Parker's A.B.C. of Gothic Architecture and some such introduction as W. R. Lethaby's Architecture or W. H. Godfrey's Story of English Architecture. From these you may pass on to such a fine work as E. S. Prior's History of Gothic Art in England or Willis and Clark's masterpiece, The Architectural History of the University of Cambridge, in which virtually the whole of English architecture is reflected in that mirror. Who will write a similar *magnum opus* for Oxford? A masterpiece is waiting to be written.

To judge from the letters that reach me, there are many people in Britain and still more in the United States who derive great pleasure from family history, particularly from the history of their own family. It is a pleasant pursuit and a door into history. The interest in the family is a prime extension of the ego : what more appealing? Naturally if it is to yield maximum satisfaction it should be an old family going back a long way, the older and more devious the better. It does not need to have been a great family, important politically, like Cecils or Howards or Russells, though such families are of more interest to the historian. To the amateur the pursuit is all the better for being not too easy, a little difficult and obscure. The older the family the more scope it gives; the more veils to be tracked down, with their tantalizing references to heirlooms and treasures all too probably vanished – but think of the amusement of recognizing them still there in a chest or jewel-box after the centuries! And the more references in parish registers to be sought out and sifted ; it is all the better if the family-tree is not too erect – a little bastardy here and there adds to its interest. There are people altruistic enough to take an interest in other people's families ; if you have no family of your own to speak of, there is an alternative. It may provide a bottom for a lasting interest in history; after all, human society consists of families.

I certainly would not discourage, I am all in favour of, the marked interest many Americans have in tracing their ancestry back in the old country. Anything that keeps the human family together is a good thing ; preserving links is not always easy, and in this case is an authentic department of scholarship. On his first visit to England Benjamin Franklin in 1758 tracked down his grandfather's gravestone in the churchyard of Ecton, Northamptonshire. George Washington came from an early medieval family of the place of that name, where the Elizabethan manor-house remains, in County Durham. The family moved to Lancashire and thence to Sulgrave in Northamptonshire, where the house of Washington's immediate ancestors in the Elizabethan age remains. The genealogy of the family has been studied fully in three stout volumes. The Somerset provenance of T. S. Eliot's family is the inspiration of his famous poem, 'East Coker' in *Four Quartets*.

When one considers how many good historical biographies there are it is surprising how few family histories there are that are works of art. Yet the family, rather than the individual, is the true unit of history. Fortunately the most famous of American families has had a good book devoted to it, J. T. Adams's *The Adams Family*. I have portrayed a comparable English family in *The Early Churchills* and *The Later Churchills*. What excellent subjects on both sides remain to be dealt with! – Roosevelts, Randolphs, Wadsworths, Rockefellers, Astors; Cecils, Russells, Howards, Cavendishes, Greys, Chamberlains.

The interest in family history is bound up with so many other delightful things : the interest of the house in which so much has taken place, the charm of its possessions, pictures, hangings, furniture, down to the maps of the estate, the stories of its ghosts. It extends to all the locality; and, as Dr J. H. Weaver tells us, there is no end to local history : 'The material of local history, in the broad sense of the word, is almost unlimited in quantity, or limited only by what is actually available in our national records as a whole.' As you see, it conforms at least to the second half of that excellent definition of a hobby – 'has no sense at all and no finality'.

It leads straight to the pleasures of archaeologizing, of pick and shovel, the esoteric excitements of the dig. Or perhaps they are not so esoteric after all – they go back to the primitive enjoyment of the treasure-hunt. Most of us share readily in the fun of a picnic-jaunt across moor and cliff in all weathers, mackintosh and sou'-wester if necessary, to cliff-camp or dolmen, to stone-circle or barrow, or some Wayland Smith's cave on the downs. Walking is best, map in hand ; sandwiches must not be forgotten – they taste better out in the open air after a long tramp. Nor must we forget that archaeology, more than any other branch of historical study, provides scope for the pleasures of hatred, malice and all uncharitableness. Anybody who knows the ways of county antiquaries knows that *odium theo-logicum* is nothing compared with *odium archaeologicum*.

A fascinating subject that has been opened up only in our own time, and in which already enormous strides have been made, is the study of English place-names. It adds to the pleasure of walking the countryside to know the derivation and meaning of the names of places you go through ; often they throw a shaft of light into the most distant past and will reveal to you the nature and origin of the place, its early settlement, the character of the whole district. So much of the documentation of our early history has perished – the place-names themselves are the most reliable documents that remain. Here you may come upon a Celtic name that reveals to you an early British settlement that went on happily among the surrounding English. There are many Waltons in various parts of the country, often, though not always, meaning just that : Welsh-towns. Or take the little finger of Saxon names along the river Ottery on the Cornish side of the Tamar pointing into that almost completely Celtic county ; surviving evidence of an English settlement on that side of the border. The study of the place-names of Devon has revealed, what we should not have known otherwise, that it was settled by West Saxons coming in from the north, from Somerset, not, as we should have supposed, from Dorset coming straight west along the coast. It does not count for nothing in their subsequent character and history that Devon and Somerset are more English and less Celtic than Dorset. Or take Cumberland and Westmorland : their place-names reveal the fact that their population springs from a mixture of Celts, Angles, Norse, with the last possibly the dominant strain ; hence that magnificent, tough, rugged stock, the dalesmen. Of such is the incomparably rich and fertile variousness of our stock made ; it is no less fascinating, though more arduous to follow their progress overseas, in the United States and Canada, Australia, New Zealand, and, to a lesser extent, South Africa.

Those great scholars, Henry Bradley (read his masterly little book, *The Making of English*) and Walter Skeat, were the founders of this study at the beginning of this century. In our time it has grown into a province of its own, in which the leaders are Sir Allen Mawer and Professor F. M. Stenton with a distinguished recruit from Scandinavia – where there is much interest in the study and whence some valuable contributions have come – Professor Eilert Ekwall. There is a society, the English Place-Name Society, devoted to it, engaged in surveying the whole country, county by county, giving a volume to each, sometimes more. You should make a point of looking up your own county in the series ; if it has not yet appeared there may be another book that covers it : many counties have been dealt with. Then read the introductory volume to the survey, which gives you an admirable guide to the subject and its methods. One cannot hope to purchase all the volumes of the survey ; but in default of that, there is an excellent alternative : *The Concise Oxford Dictionary of English Place-Names* (by Professor Ekwall).

For the United States there is a most attractive way of studying this subject with George R. Stewart's *Names on the Land*. Through this one can follow the belts of settlement across the American continent, and the different sections that settled it at various periods – the original Indian names, often the most beautiful and haunting, the Spanish, always charming, the English, Dutch and, in old Louisiana (as in Quebec), French. As one follows the process of settlement in the names, one feels how it takes up the movement of the peoples that populated Britain a thousand years before.

Military and naval history are important subjects in themselves, the study of which has received a great impulse with the wars of the twentieth century – and in consequence an immense growth in the literature devoted to them. They have always had their devotees since the time of Julius Caesar, whose *Commentaries on the Gallic War* remains a classic example of the subject. Among British historians Sir Charles Oman wrote a *History of the Art of War in the Middle Ages*, and followed it with a volume on the sixteenth century, the Renaissance developments in the art. On war, in and for itself, the classic treatment is that of the German Clausewitz, a hard nut to crack. For the beginner the best approach remains the biographical : such works as Sir Winston Churchill's *Life and Times of Marl-*

borough, Guedalla's *Wellington*, the one-volume edition of Douglas S. Freeman's *Robert E. Lee*, edited by R. B. Harwell. Excellent, sympathetic treatments of their subjects are to be found in the books of Cyril Falls, *A Hundred Years of War*, *The First World War*, *The Second World War*.

A famous introduction to naval history is Admiral Mahan's *The Influence of Sea-Power on History*. He also wrote the standard study of *Nelson and British Sea-Power*. For the founder of the U.S. naval tradition, read S. E. Morison's *Paul Jones*. This eminent historian has written, practically singlehanded, the official history of the U.S. Navy in the second world war. The official British history is a cooperative effort. Again, on the biographical side, one should certainly read S. E. Morison's *Christopher Columbus*; also J. A. Williamson's *Sir Francis Drake and Hawkins of Plymouth*, perhaps my *Sir Richard Grenville*, and, for the fullest biography of Nelson on the personal side, Carola Oman's *Nelson*. Garrett Mattingly's brilliant book, *The Defeat of the Spanish Armada*, combines the naval story with the political and diplomatic in an original and satisfying synthesis.

Also of growing interest in our time is the history of ideas, though the nineteenth century produced classics in this field, such as Leslie Stephen's *History of English Thought in the Eighteenth Century*, and *The English Utilitarians*. E. Halévy's *Formation of Philosophical Radicalism* is a fine work; V. L. Parrington's *Main Currents in American Thought*, like all the work of Charles Beard, less satisfactory; partisan and politically motivated, therefore impermanent.

Far more valuable was the idea that Frederick Jackson Turner put forward in his essay on 'The Frontier in American History'. This has had a remarkable and fertilizing influence, not only in American historiography but beyond the frontiers, in other countries.

No less influential in its day was Buckle's original *History of Civilisation in England*. The history of theological speculation may be regarded as part of the history of ideas; but Burckhardt warns us that Buckle's intensive study of the Scottish divines of the seventeenth century cost him a paralysis of the brain.

Better, more rewarding, is the concrete study of time and place. In the end, as always in history, we come back to that experience we call the 'moment of illumination'. It is nowhere better described than by Browning:

> On the arch where olives overhead
>   Print the blue sky with twig and leaf
> (That sharp-curled leaf which they never shed)
>   Twixt the aloes, I used to lean in chief,
> And mark through the winter afternoons,
>   By a gift God grants me now and then,
> In the mild decline of those suns like moons,
>   Who walked in Florence, besides her men.

8   How to
Teach Yourself History

You might think that in order to learn history you need a library of books to begin with. Not at all ; that only comes at the end. What you need at the beginning is a pair of stout walking shoes, a pencil and a notebook ; perhaps I should add a good county guide covering the area you mean to explore – I find Methuen's *Little Guides* most useful – and a map of the country, preferably a one-inch Ordnance Survey that gives you field footpaths and a wealth of things of interest, marks churches and historic buildings and ruins, wayside crosses and holy wells, prehistoric camps and dykes, the sites of battles. When you can't go for a walk it is quite a good thing to study the map and plan where you would like to go. I am all in favour of the open-air approach to history : the most delightful and enjoyable, the most imaginative and informative, and – what not everybody understands – the best training.

This is the true countryman's approach, and it has many advantages, especially in understanding the early history of the island. You might take Jacquetta Hawkes's delightful book *Early Britain* (Collins's 'Britain in Pictures' series), with its beautiful illustrations, and graduate from that to V. Gordon Childe's *Prehistoric Communities of the British Isles*. The first of these is enough to equip you to tackle the prehistoric ridgeways and tracks that exist all over the country and offer the best walking, springy turf, air like wine, a blessed release from the noise and traffic of the modern world – only the larks and nowadays (alas !) the planes. The distinguished archaeologist, Dr O. G. S. Crawford, tells us that countrymen understand best, almost instinctively, the conditions of prehistoric life, and that the proceedings of small country field-clubs are often far ahead of the leading archaeological journals in the true appreciation of pre-historic problems. This is the man who in our time has demon-strated by air photography the Celtic system of agriculture, with its small fields on the uplands, that was brought to an end by the English who cleared the forests and river valleys. You can still see the traces of that earlier upland cultivation revealed in the air photographs. (Look them up in that agreeable journal, *Antiquity*.)

In prehistoric times Britain was covered with a system of up-land communications: 'The ridgeways and harrow-ways that connected the hill-top forts and the Celtic villages formed a system of communications the excellence of which we are only now beginning to appreciate.' So writes Mr Randall in his *History in the Open Air*; his essay on 'The Old Roads of England' is an excellent aid to a good road-sense; I mean, of course, an historic sense of the road, not just how to drive a car. He shows us how to keep a weather-eye open, for 'an existing bit of road may be partly prehistoric, partly Roman, partly medieval and partly modern'; and he gives us two valuable clues to follow: 'the capital distinction is between the roads that grew and the roads that were made. . . . Secondly, the age of a road is deter-mined by the earliest monuments or objects found in definite relation to it.' Mr Belloc, who is not to be trusted as an historian – he is so full of prejudice and *parti pris* – nevertheless has a fine sense of topography and an eye for the road; and I recom-mend his account of the old Pilgrims' road to Canterbury, *The Old Road*, in spite of its mistakes, as an example of the right approach and the right feeling for roads.

There ought to be similar books for our waterways – rivers and canals. What delightful books are waiting to be written in this field, or, perhaps I should say, in these waters. So far as the rivers are concerned, the emphasis might be on the Middle Ages and the medieval towns along their routes. Mr Randall tells us: 'The Thames is navigable at least to Lechlade, and before the digging of the canals it was navigable to Cricklade. From these points the journey over the Cotswold country to the Severn, or either of the Avons, would be a matter of two or three days even for fairly heavy loads. It is sometimes made a matter of wonder how goods were transported along foundrous medieval roads in cumbersome medieval carts. The answer is that for the most part they went by water.' Here too we have a guide in Mr Belloc's *Historic Thames*, and a model for what may be done for other rivers, Severn and Trent, Tyne and Tees and the various Avons. We have a classic canal-book in Stevenson's *An Inland Voyage*. To the pleasures of walking we add those of canoeing and exploring our waterways by steamer and barge and boat. Nor are the railways – most characteristic product of the high Industrial Revolution – without their historic interest. I suggest as an introduction C. E. R. Sherrington's *A Hundred Years of Inland Transport*, from which one may rise to a full-dress history like W. W. Tomlinson's *History of the North-Eastern Railway*. Railways have their fans, and their fascination, no less than roads and rivers.

The townsman too has his advantages, especially if he lives in an old town, or a town that still has something old about it : if he keeps his eyes open there is more for him to see – more, I mean, that is worth seeing. Most English towns of any size have had books written about them that will serve as guides to their past and tell you what there is of interest in them : inquire at the local library or bookshop, particularly if the latter is an old business going back several generations. Nothing more delightful to discover in a town – one of the pleasures of going to a country town is searching out and savouring the local bookshops ; there is as much art in it as in wine-tasting. There is an enchanting introduction to English *Cities and Small Towns* by a writer of originality and talent, John Betjeman. Everything by this writer is to be read, thought over and absorbed ; his books are brief, but they are the works of a poet with an acute sense of the past and an infallible eye. Read also his *Vintage London* and *An Oxford University Chest*. There is an admirable old *Historic Towns* series to pick up second-hand, edited by the historian Freeman, one of whose strongest points was his sense of topography. His travel sketch-books of towns abroad, in Normandy and Main, in Provence and Sicily, are the most agreeable things that this rather disagreeable old person ever wrote. Take as an example of the method to follow in studying an historic town a recent book: *English City: The Growth and Future of Bristol*; or Geoffrey Martin, *The Town*, in Jack Simmons's new series, 'The Visual History of Britain'. With the aid of books like these you get an idea of the lay-out and growth of a city, its vital parts and organic functions: the place begins to come clear to your mind and to live for you as a place, with a personality of its own, no longer a mere passive, unnoticed background to contemporary life.

So too for English counties with their diversity of character and inexhaustible treasures of interest. It is probable that, for its area, Britain has more variety of landscape and scene than any other country in the world. Oxford stands at the gates of four quite different landscapes, and is itself characteristic of a fifth: the wooded slopes of the Chilterns, the bare lines of the Berkshire downs, the Cotswold uplands and valleys, the quiet rolling country of North Oxfordshire; the city itself a Thames valley town. An enduring feature in English history is the difference between one county and another. Think of the differences between next-door neighbours, in temperament, dialect, character of the people, landscape, between Cornwall and Devon, Devon and Dorset, Dorset and Wilts and so through all the southern counties; or between Lancashire and Yorkshire, Cumberland and Northumberland. Anyone who is to understand England must understand this, in addition to the fact that in these islands there are four different countries: England, Wales, Scotland, Ireland. Most fortunate diversity, chief source of our creativeness.*

More more could be made of county history in the schools. An admirable example of how it should be done is Mr Alec Macdonald's *Worcestershire in English History*. From these popular introductory works one can move on to magnificent quarries of material and information: to the *Victoria County Histories*, for example, of which we may cite that of Lancashire

---

* The creative effects of diversity and fusion within the islands are the leading theme of my book, *The Spirit of English History*.

as a model and the most complete. Then there are the fine volumes, with their illustrations, of the Historical Monuments Commission: surveys of the country, county by county, with all that is of archaeological and historical interest in them. There is an admirable little series of *Regional Guides* to Ancient Monuments in the care of the Ministry of Works (Stationery Office). From all this one may move back, or on, to the older standard histories of the counties, of which we may cite Hoare's *Wiltshire* and Ormerod's *Cheshire* as classic examples. An additional attraction is the characteristic engravings and prints with which these older volumes are embellished; satisfying and agreeable in themselves, they are often of houses now vanished or of views all too disagreeably changed. Many counties have their own archaeological and historical societies, with Journals and Proceedings that have been going for many years and contain a great deal of valuable and fascinating material. Let me cite only the *Transactions of the Devonshire Association* as a good example. Other societies exist to publish chiefly documents, like the Oxford Historical Society, or, for the North Country, the Surtees and Chetham Societies.

Just as it is difficult for Americans to envisage the smallness of England – it is one-third the area of California, one-fourth that of Texas – so it is hardly possible for English people to appreciate imaginatively the immense size of the United States. One cannot imagine America; one has to see it to appreciate it properly. After all, it is not like a normal European country; it is a whole continent in itself.

To help to appreciate it historically and visually, I propose the same technique as I have outlined for Britain. One may take each state, though so much larger, as historically comparable to an English county. Wherever I am in the United States I like to have a good historical guide to the particular State I am in, and fortunately there is an excellent series of W.P.A. (Works Program Aid) guides, dating from the 1930s. Naturally the older States of the east are fullest of historic interest, historical monuments and places to visit – such States as Massachusetts, New York, Pennsylvania, Virginia. Hardly less full of historic interest are States such as California, Connecticut, South Carolina, Illinois. But every State, even the most recent, has sóme historic interest, beside the geographical and visual, the attractions of scenery.

A second principle I recommend is to use a good history of the particular State you happen to be in – preferably in one volume, such as T. C. Pease's excellent history of Illinois, or R. G. Cleland's *From Wilderness to Empire: A History of California, 1542–1900*. And there are more detailed studies, such as C. E. Chapman's volume on Spanish California. These are only good specimens taken from an immense field ; impossible to mention more.

The general point is, though it is hardly realized, that there is as much interest in regional and local history in the United States as in Britain. Every State has its historical society, some of them with famous series of publications to their credit, like the Massachusetts and Virginia Historical Societies.

Historic towns have good volumes devoted to them – compare the admirable books devoted to Philadelphia by a foremost such scholar, Howard D. Eberlein. Or such books as Paul Horgan's *Santa Fé*. One can learn a great deal of American history from the novels of so judicious and discriminating a writer, imbued with the sense of history, as Willa Cather – read her *Death Comes for the Archbishop* for the Spanish south-west, *Shadows on the Rock* for Quebec, *My Antonía* for Nebraska, *Sapphira and the Slave Girl* for Virginia.

For the story of a famous road read George R. Stewart's *Highway 40*. There should be more such, as well as histories of the most famous railroads and other routes, and historic rivers. A classic story of a celebrated route across the continent is Parkman's *The Oregon Trail*. All Parkman's books have the sap of life in them – he is the most original of American historians. Not far behind comes Prescott, with his *Conquest of Mexico* and the *Conquest of Peru*, as fresh and readable as when written. Henry Adams is a more curious case as an historian ; *The Education of Henry Adams* is a work of genius, so is his *Mont St Michel and Chartres* ; but his history of the administrations of Madison and Monroe is disfigured by a bias unworthy of one who considered himself so much more objective than others.

There are three golden rules, it seems to me :

1. KEEP YOUR EYES OPEN.
2. TAKE NOTES.
3. READ THE RIGHT BOOKS.

The first of these I have dealt with. The second implies the third, and I must explain the art of taking notes. It is not only from books that one takes notes; one may take notes from lectures, or notes of things seen or observed. If you are to teach yourself history you should always have a notebook at hand, or carry a small one in your pocket. Into that enter the things of interest you want to remember ; it may be an inscription on a monument, or useful date (there has been nothing in this book about dates, that bugbear of the anti-historical), a building or some object you may want to know more about or of which you want to remember the appearance : or it may be the name of a book, a quotation, or some passage you fancy ; or a note of some portrait or picture in a gallery. Get into the habit of visiting picture galleries and museums when you can ; they give an interesting slant on history, their contents are part of the life of the past, so much treasure-trove cast up by the tide of time.

The art of taking notes from lectures is the same as that of making notes from books ; the salient point is to get down the gist of the thing. It is possible to take too many notes ; Lord Acton took so many that he never could get on with his writing, and his famous Inaugural Lecture is a nightmare of quotations ; it makes one feel that at some time or other someone has thought of everything. What you will find is that at the beginning of your reading you will need to take more notes than later on. At first much that you read will be new to you and you will want to memorize it ; later on, as your reading grows, the picture will fill in for you ; partly consciously and partly unconsciously, a deposit of knowledge will accumulate and you will need to take fewer notes ; you will already know something of what you are reading and will need to note only what is new. On the basis of what you have read before *plus* your own sense you may be able in time to criticize what you are reading. At the beginning it is a good idea to try to summarize the gist of each paragraph of what you are reading into one sentence, or at most two; and in addition to take down any striking passage or phrase you may want to quote *verbatim*.

A word on the books you should read. *It is most important always to read the best books you can on a subject.* Beginners hardly realize how important this is; but you may be given quite a wrong view of a subject by starting off on the wrong footing. Most of the nonsense that is talked about history by people who don't know comes from their reading trash on the subject. Take, for example, the absurd popular ideas about Henry VIII and Queen Elizabeth: you should read A. F. Pollard's biography of Henry, not Francis Hackett's; Sir John Neale's *Queen Elizabeth* and Elizabeth Jenkins's *Elizabeth the Great*, not Belloc's or Theodore Maynard's stuff about her. It is here that tutors and lecturers can be most useful, in putting you on to the best books to read; after all, the reading you must do for yourself. But if you are very much on your own, as most people are, there is no reason to be downcast or despairing; for once you get on the track of the right reading, you will build up a critical knowledge for yourself that will tell you what is sense and what is nonsense.

*

It may be thought that I have lost sight of the history of the country as such. Not at all; I have had it in mind all the time. As I have said, the mental world of the average, even intelligent, man is largely limited to his own country; he does not enter intimately or in any significant way into the languages and cultures of others. The history of his own country therefore has a central importance and he needs to begin by getting an adequate picture of that. Perhaps I may be forgiven for suggesting my *Spirit of English History* as an introduction, since it is the briefest possible. It is only an introduction, intended as a summing up of what our history comes to and to show how it has developed on the lines it has, so differently from other European countries. It must be followed by a book on a bigger scale with more scope for detailed treatment; the best is G. M. Trevelyan's *History of England*. This may be followed by J. A. Williamson's

Great Britain and the Empire. Having arrived at this point one can fill out the picture with Trevelyan's *English Social History*.

One might think it safe to launch out now on the classics of historical writing: Macaulay, Carlyle, Froude; Clarendon, Hume, Gibbon. But not quite yet. These for the most part deal with definite periods; and it is better to get an idea of those periods in terms of modern scholarship first; you will get things in a better perspective, be able to discount their bias, note their prejudices and avoid their mistakes. For example, for the six-teenth century you should read Fisher's and Pollard's volumes in 'Longman's History of England', together with Neale's *Elizabeth* and Williamson's *The Age of Drake*. Then you can go on to Froude's *History of England*. Similarly for the seventeenth century: first read Trevelyan's *England under the Stuarts*, Sir George Clark's *The Later Stuarts* in the new 'Oxford History of England' and Trevelyan's *England under Queen Anne*; then go on to Macaulay.

This may be thought timid counsel, for, after all, the great historians have far more to offer in the end than lesser writers: imaginative power, literary gifts that enable them to re-create where others just plod along after the facts, a deeper insight into the ways of men, more knowledge of the world – in a word, genius. Nor are they ever afraid to say what they think. I am only providing here for the beginner; later on he will be able to read the classics with all the more understanding. At the beginning he needs someone to warn him as to the particular bias and prejudices of a given writer.

Take, for example, the greatest of English historians, Gibbon. He has two grave defects. He can never do justice to Christianity and what it did achieve – the civilization of the barbarians, for one thing. Because he could not accept its supernatural claims, the author of *The Decline and Fall of the Roman Empire* seizes every opportunity to denigrate the Church and its adherents and to present them in a ridiculous light: the book is full of sly remarks, subacid inflections, dubious jokes, pin-pricks. Very amusing, very naughty; but, strictly from an historian's point of view, rather shocking. He ought to have been fair and im-partial, whereas with him the case – and the joke – always goes against the Christians. Not to appreciate their good work in the world, along with the bad, the marvellous achievements of the Church along with its failures and misdeeds, is in itself unhistorical. Then, too, he is very unjust to the Byzantine empire, which represents a remarkable positive achievement that Gibbon seems to have been unaware of; for a thousand years it stood on guard at the gate of European civilization against the Turks, and even then would not have fallen if it had not been irretrievably weakened by the disgraceful onslaught of the West in the Latin Crusade. Gibbon was obsessed, not unreasonably, by the folly of mankind; he thought that history 'is, indeed, little more than the register of the crimes, follies, and misfortunes of mankind'. This is only one side of the picture; too much of the splendid canvas he painted is in eighteenth-century chiaroscuro. He had no sense of the spiritual achievement of man. But that is only to say that he was the child of his age, of that age of enlightenment, of scepticism and disillusion. All the same, his defects are nothing compared with his gifts and qualities : to read him is an education in itself.

With a general picture of English history in mind, you can then branch out in two directions. On the one hand you can follow up the periods and subjects of English history that interest you in greater detail; on the other you can make it your aim to get some idea of general European history. Once you have gone a certain way with the latter and got a firm outline in mind, it is a good thing to work the two together to some extent. Let me make this clear by illustration. H. A. L. Fisher's *History of Europe* will give you a good outline of the story of European civilization from ancient Greece onwards; probably the most convenient introduction, liberal, old-fashioned, humane. I think it desirable also to get the hang of prehistory: read Sir John Myres's brilliant little book, *The Dawn of History*, and two of Gordon Childe's, *Man Makes Himself* and *What Happened in History*. You might follow these with one or two books that cover whole periods: Warde Fowler's *Rome*, R. W. Southern's *The Making of the Middle Ages*, J. H. Plumb's *The Renaissance*, Sir George Clark's *The Seventeenth Century*, Bertrand Russell's *Freedom and Organisation in the Nineteenth*

Century. Then you can go in more detail into some particular period. I agree with Bury's view that it is practically more important for people to know about the most recent period of history, that which provides the background to events today, which has such a dominating influence upon our own lives. It is here that the two strands come together: while you are reading English history you must see it in relation to the European and world environment.

The last volume in the new 'Oxford History', R. C. K. Ensor's *England 1870–1914*, is a first-class survey of the events leading up to our own time: stimulating at every point, very wide in its sympathies, fresh-minded and original. No one could possibly find history anything but fascinating if written like that. Or, for the whole century, there is Trevelyan's *British History in the Nineteenth Century*. These books telling us what was happening here should be read along with those describing events abroad, both in Europe and beyond. For France, read D. W. Brogan's *The Development of Modern France*; for Germany, A. J. P. Taylor's *The Course of German History*; both independent-minded, trenchant, thought-provoking. For Russia, read B. H. Sumner's *Survey of Russian History*, rather more difficult, for it is an original attempt at a new method, to read history back from the situation today; but a strikingly impartial treatment of a notoriously controversial subject. For the United States, read Allan Nevins's concise *Brief History of the United States* and go on to Morison and Commager's fine survey, *The Growth of the American Republic*. For the European background as a whole I might suggest Croce's *History of Europe in the Nineteenth Century*, and Alison Phillips's *Modern Europe*. The two strands may be usefully brought together in R. W. Seton-Watson's *Britain in Europe, 1789–1914*.

From now on, with such a general framework of history in mind, you will be able to fill it out wherever you choose, in the most congenial manner possible, by reading historical biographies. With such a firm framework to go upon there will be no danger of getting them out of chronological order, or out of proportion in the general perspective. In any case there is a remedy: to read biographies on both sides of historical conflicts,

Strafford as well as Cromwell, Hamilton alongside Jefferson, Gladstone as well as Disraeli, Lincoln beside Jefferson Davis and Robert E. Lee, Stalin *and* Trotsky. Let me give a few examples only of the biographical approach. Let us take Napoleon. You could not do better than begin with H. A. L. Fisher's brilliant little *Napoleon*, and go on to Fournier's standard biography in two volumes. But you should get the point of view of his critics and opponents too ; read also, therefore, Duff-Cooper's *Talleyrand*, Algernon Cecil's *Metternich*, Holland Rose's *Life of William Pitt* ; then go on to Mathiez's *History of the French Revolution* and J. M. Thompson's *French Revolution*. In the end you should graduate with Sorel's classic, *L'Europe et la Révolution Française*.

Or again for the English nineteenth century, you might begin with Lytton Strachey's *Queen Victoria*, Philip Guedalla's *The Duke* and his *Palmerston*, and go on to G. M. Young's *Early Victorian England*, Moneypenny and Buckle's *Disraeli* and Morley's *Gladstone*.

This is becoming too much of a bibliography ; my excuse is that these are only illustrations of the method of historical reading. And I have indicated enough to start you off on your way ; you should be able to go forward on your own steam now. These books will have their own bibliographies and references to other books in which to follow up what interests you. And you will by now have developed, almost unconsciously, a critical sense that will help you to pick and choose. This will be needed when you come to tackle large works of corporate scholarship like the Cambridge Histories, Ancient, Medieval and Modern, the Cambridge History of the British Empire, of British Foreign Policy and so on. For the most important fact about these works is that you are not expected to read them right through – nobody could – but to pick out the chapters that are germane to your subject ; they differ very much in quality. In fact you have learnt to *use* books as well as to read them for pleasure.

Looking out for the books you want is itself a pleasure, occasionally heightened by expectancy and sharpened by irritation at not finding them. The delights of book-collecting are well known and have often been celebrated. What more agreeable pursuit than bookshop-crawling? A pleasure for which one has much to show in the end ; a well-stocked library and, I hope, a well-stocked mind.

As for historical research, in the pure sense of the word, I have said little of it directly, for that is a subject of its own, of a specialist character. And there are various standard works to which you can refer, covering the subject − such as Langlois and Seignobos's *Introduction to the Study of History* and C. G. Crump's *History and Historical Research*. There is an admirable series of S.P.C.K. pamphlets too, 'Helps for Students of History', now unfortunately out of print, but sometimes obtainable second-hand. On the subject of writing history I have said nothing at all ; for its pleasures and excitements, rare and esoteric, simple and satisfying, I refer you to that revealing masterpiece, Gibbon's *Autobiography*.

In truth, the writing of history, with the subsidiary subject of historical research and how to do it, demands a whole book in itself.

Index

More about Penguins and Pelicans

Penguinews, which appears every month, contains details of all the new books issued by Penguins as they are published. From time to time it is supplemented by *Penguins in Print*, which is a complete list of all books published by Penguins which are in print. (There are well over three thousand of these.)

A specimen copy of *Penguinews* will be sent to you free on request, and you can become a subscriber for the price of the postage. For a year's issues (including the complete lists) please send 25p if you live in the United Kingdom, or 50p if you live elsewhere. Just write to Dept EP, Penguin Books Ltd, Harmondsworth, Middlesex, enclosing a cheque or postal order, and your name will be added to the mailing list.

Some other books published by Penguins are described on the following pages.

Note : *Penguinews* and *Penguins in Print* are not available in the U.S.A. or Canada

a Pelican book

What is History?

E. H. Carr

'Simply to show how it really was.' Ranke, stating what he considered the proper aim of the historian, filled generations of historians after him with a burning zeal for objectivity.

But who is to say how things were? In formulating a modern answer to the question *What is History?* Professor Carr shows that the 'facts' of history are simply those which historians have selected for scrutiny. Millions have crossed the Rubicon, but the historians tell us that only Caesar's crossing was significant. All historical facts come to us as a result of interpretative choices by historians influenced by the standards of their age.

Yet if absolute objectivity is impossible, the role of the historian need in no way suffer, nor does history lose its fascination. Indeed, this published version of the 1961 Trevelyan Lectures at Cambridge confirms the vitality of both.

'E. H. Carr, author of the monumental *History of Soviet Russia*, now proves himself to be not only our most distinguished modern historian but also one of the most valuable contributors to historical theory' – *Spectator*

Not for sale in the U.S.A.

The Early Churchills

A. L. Rowse

From obscure beginnings in the West Country to the death of Sarah, the remarkable first Duchess of Marlborough, A. L. Rowse traces the foundations of one of England's greatest families.

Here we meet the original Sir Winston Churchill, the Cavalier colonel, described by his famous descendant as one of the most notable and potent of sires; his daughter Arabella, mistress of James II and mother of the martial Duke of Berwick, his eldest son John, the Duke of Marlborough, who curbed the ambitions of Louis XIV; and other Churchills who left their mark on English history.

The Early Churchills to quote the *Listener* 'sets a model for family history . . . a brilliant example'

Not for sale in the U.S.A.